JA 18 '01

Dakota Circle
Excursions on the True Plains

By Tom Isern

**Institute for Regional Studies,
North Dakota State University, Fargo.**

Dedication

To the people of the Great Plains, God bless them
(and that's not just a rhetorical convention).

Introduction, compilation, and format of essays
© 2000
Institute for Regional Studies,
North Dakota State University, Fargo, ND 58105

Original newspaper columns composing essays ©Plains Folk.

International Standard Book Number (ISBN) 0-911042-53-9.

Library of Congress Catalog Card Number 00-104613

Dakota Circle

Contents

1. Dakota Circle

Dakota Circle–whence this cryptic title? There are several potential explanations. Tipi rings, for instance. Throughout the northern plains, wherever rocky shoulders overlook level bottoms, local residents are likely to point out the presence of these lithic artifacts. Tipi rings lend the aura of antiquity to a locality. They are mute to persons lacking imagination, but whole persons cannot fail to be moved by the wholeness of the geometric form. Were I to say the title of this book refers to these mystic rings from the aboriginal past, it would be appealing to the new-age market.

That would be a good story, or I could make up a few others, but the truth is that the title comes from the commonplace behaviors of ordinary and marvelous people of the present in this part of the country. One pattern of behavior in particular.

If you're from North Dakota or Dakota Territory, you may not notice this any more, but if you're from somewhere else, it's intriguing. Invite over a group of country folk from around here, and you find that they don't have the knack for cocktail-party behavior. People are supposed to mingle and converse, break up and reform, chat and argue, right? Well, they don't.

And you can't make them. You can set up the bar in one room, and the crock pot full of little weenies with barbeque sauce (the mark of elegant entertaining in Dakota Territory) in another, and spread finger food and dips and cakes and cookies all over the place, but this will not lead people to disperse about the house the way they are supposed to.

No, they will mill around for a while and then gravitate to some room that will hold all of them, bringing their plates and chairs with them, and arrange themselves into what I call the Dakota Circle. No one can be in the middle. All must be on the periphery, where everyone can see everyone.

This is comfortable. With everyone present and accounted for, you know no one is talking about you behind your back.

Well, that's putting it too negative. There is a wonderful democracy and dignity in the Dakota Circle. Topics are raised and addressed in due course, beginning with the weather, and moving on to the food.

When talk comes to matters of substance, the patterns of community emerge. A question is posed, and the Dakotans look at one another across and around the Dakota Circle until an unspoken consensus is forged as to who should answer the question. Modestly, the appropriate person speaks to the matter, and the others listen. When she has told as much as she should, she pitches the ball to a neighbor by saying something like, "Howard, you were there, is that the way you remember it?" From there on, if others feel comfortable, the conversation proceeds like a skip-passing warm-up drill at a Class B basketball game. Eventually everyone has the opportunity to catch and pass.

This is the sort of thing I noticed when my wife and I moved from Kansas to North Dakota in 1992. Kansas and North Dakota are both plains states, states with strongly agricultural and extractive economies (they take turns leading the country in wheat production), states predominantly settled by northern Europeans, states with similar east-west complementarities and tensions (eastern Kansas vs. everyone west of Highway 81, Imperial Cass vs. the rest of the state). I expected to see mainly cultural similarities between my native state and my new home. The similarities were there, as the two states share in plains regional culture, but to my surprise, the dissimilarities were stark.

This is not the place for me to try to be definitive about the differences or to explain them with certainty, but I think most people who are familiar with the southern plains and with the northern plains would accept some tentative dichotomies. People of the south are brash, those of the north reserved; people of the south relish risk, those of the north crave security; people of the south brag about their home towns, those of the north deprecate theirs; people of the south insult you to your face (sometimes as a form of affection), those of the north hold it in; people of the south join in singing "Home on the Range," those of the north won't sing anything unless you can tell them the page number in the hymnal.

Hofva Lutheran Church, Steele County, Dakota.

Why are these two camps of plains folk so different? Some explanations are ready, and I think that in combination, they go a long way. Ethnicity and religion are factors, certainly. Evangelical Norwegian

Lutheranism lies
thick as a snow
bank across the
north and east of
North Dakota,
while German-
Russian village
culture percolates
up from the south
and west. Each of
these two dominant
groups contributes
its own style of
reserve, and the
antipathy between

St. Joseph Catholic Church, Grant County,
North Dakota.

Courtesy State Historical Society of North Dakota.

the two accentuates it. The economic situation of the
northern plains also has its cultural effect, I think. The
colonial status of the region gives rise to an us-against-all-of-
them attitude and to a culture of guerrilla resistance that
teeters on the edge between a constructive survival strategy
and a destructively negative mind set. Perhaps the most
dismaying aspect of northern plains regional culture is its
cultural cringe toward Minneapolis, with the attendant
depreciation of all that is indigenous.

Despite these potent human determinants, eventually
the land has its way with people, space becomes place, and
viable, even elegant patterns of culture emerge. People stand
more squarely on their own feet, they speak for themselves,
they build structures that back up their words, and they
relate to one another in the fashion of a community. This is
a work in progress. Contrary to the classic tenets of grasslands ecology, balance and stability never happen. That

makes it all the more interesting to watch the process, to observe and note how people are getting along with the land and making their place in it.

Which is what the newspaper column, *Plains Folk*, is about. *Dakota Circle* is substantially a book of essays drawn from *Plains Folk*, a weekly column about life on the Great Plains of North America. The column has been distributed and published in unbroken weekly sequence since April 1983. My co-author is Jim Hoy of Emporia State University; the nature of the co-authorship is that we alternate weeks, he writing the odd-numbered columns and I the even. The column is self-syndicated for distribution to newspapers on the southern plains.

As an amplification and offshoot of this continuing series, the NDSU Extension Service commenced distribution of my *Plains Folk* columns in 1995. This weekly distribution drew on archival columns; on new columns being written for the continuing numbered series; and, increasingly, on new, additional columns dealing specifically with North Dakota and neighboring states and provinces that I wrote specifically for the Extension release. The Extension distribution of my *Plains Folk* columns results in their appearance in from thirty-five to forty newspapers each week. *Dakota Circle* is a re-working of material that has appeared in this fashion, along with additional material that has come to light, often through the kindnesses of readers. The photos placed with the essays–I took them myself on my excursions.

Here come the credits, beginning with the tightest circle, my own household. Many of the excursions recounted in this book were shared with my darling Lotte, who was, indeed, an active collaborator in some of the work. She has my thanks and my heart. I don't think she would mind sharing this paragraph with my other erstwhile companion in field work, the late Bancroft the History Dog, famous for his nose and his heart and especially for the day he took a bite out of the Dean of Business.

North Dakota State University is a wonderful base for my sort of work. I have a sympathetic dean, Tom Riley, and supportive friends in the Department of History, including a fine chairman, Larry Peterson; a splendid co-worker in the vineyard of agricultural history, Dave Danbom; and my favorite target for harassment, John Helgeland. In NDSU Libraries I have imposed a great deal on Larry Schwartz (formerly of NDSU, now of Moorhead State University), Fran Fisher, John Bye, and Mike Robinson, and they are good to me. The Institute for Regional Studies is a great institutional asset and a personal boon for me. Within NDSU Extension it was Barry Brissman who first suggested a North Dakota series of *Plains Folk*, and I'm grateful for his confidence; Dean Hulse now handles my work for Extension with sensitivity and sense. Two talented and loyal staff people who have helped to keep my university life in good order through the years are Cathy Heiraas and Pam Murphy, whom I probably have not thanked often enough. In general I delight in my association with a great land-grant university of the Great Plains. Its values of accessibility and practicality are my own; it is grounded in the land and people of the plains, as am I.

The research behind certain parts of this book was supported by granting agencies. The Canadian work, for instance, comes by way of generous grants from the Embassy of Canada. In that regard I also should mention that the Canadian Plains Research Center, University of Regina, has been of material assistance throughout my various sojourns on the Canadian prairies. The Bowman County work here described was supported by the State Historical Society of North Dakota, which provided a grant from its Preservation Services Fund. My thanks to all these parties for their confidence and support.

Most of all, though, I want to express my thanks, respect, and affection for the people of the plains and especially the plains folk of North Dakota. A tenured professorship is a public trust deserving my best labors and loyalties. I hope you like the work I do for you, in this book and elsewhere. You may not like everything I say, but you know that I care about this place.

"Place," I just said. That's what this book is about, a place. I'm not here to argue fine points or push grand theses. Careful readers will notice some strong themes threaded through the work, and I hope you will chew on them, but that's ancillary to the main purpose of the book. The main purpose of the book is not conversion, but delight. The Great Plains are a neat place. We need to remind one another of that now and then.

So, fill your plates and scoot your chairs into the living room, make room there for the others to get in. Everyone settled? All right, let's get started.

2. What Are Plains Like?

Because I grew up on a wheat farm in western Kansas and have lived all my life on the plains of Kansas, Oklahoma, Texas, Nebraska, Saskatchewan, and North Dakota, I'm accustomed to open country. Mountains are all right, I guess, because you can get on top of them and get a good view of the plains. Trees I don't care for. Now and then my otherwise-sensible wife gets a wild hair and starts talking about going on a fall foliage excursion somewhere. This, to me, would be the Inferno.

When we have visitors here in the Red River Valley, they always marvel (or mourn) how "flat" it is. And I always correct them, letting them know that the appropriate usage is "level."

The greatest of Great Plains historians, Walter P. Webb, said that the Great Plains are level, treeless, and semiarid–a fair likeness. His choice of adjectives focuses on physical geography, however, and says nothing of the human culture of the plains.

I've been teaching college courses on the history and culture of the plains for many years, and I used to start out by asking the students, "What are the Great Plains?" That didn't work, because they kept telling me where the plains are, instead of what they are.

So now I say, "Give me three adjectives to describe the Great Plains." This works much better. For instance, I went through the exercise one autumn with thirty NDSU students, most of them from North Dakota, a minority from Minnesota, and a scattering from bordering states. I thought you might be interested in what adjectives they applied to our country.

"Flat" or "level" won out, with sixteen mentions. Closely related were the seven mentions of "open" or "wide-open," along with the twelve instances of "big," "large," "vast," "wide," or "expansive." Then there were the other expected responses—"prairie," "grassland," "tree-less," or "grassy" (nine references along these lines) and "windy" or "wind-swept" (six of these).

Broken windows of a consolidated school in Bowman County, North Dakota, stare out on a depopulated landscape.

Things get real interesting when you scan the list of adjectives that are outliers—ones that don't fit the typical pattern. Quite a number of these are unfavorable: plain, brown, dusty, isolated, barren, desolate, dry. It's a hard country, no doubt.

Parallel to these, often coming from the same people, is another list that portrays the plains as a wholesome heart-land: rolling, progressive, peaceful, plentiful, productive, small-town, historic, and even beautiful. Mixed feelings abound.

Then you come to the most intriguing catalog of adjectives—those that have to do not with the senses, nor with the heart, but with the spirit. These adjectives are a window on the soul: turbulent, volatile, exciting, dangerous, frontier-like, roaming, extreme, breath-taking, rugged, and–my favorite of all–mysterious.

Who wrote that word, "mysterious"? Was it some young horseman who stumbled into a tipi ring on a Souris River hilltop? Was it some young woman who found her grandmother's cryptic diary? Was it some young person marveling at the abandoned homesteads, boarded-up schools, gray-faded main streets, and other archeological remains of an earlier civilization never to be experienced by the new generation on the plains?

Who wrote that word, "mysterious"?

A few years ago my erstwhile co-author, Jim Hoy, wrote a column, "The Allure of the Plains," that a lot of people liked. In it he confessed that mountains made him claustrophobic and he didn't much care for trees. "Plains folk," he said, "take space and openness for granted."

My mother, native to Barton County, Kansas, cut out that column and stuck it under a magnet on her refrigerator. She never did that with any of my columns.

I did get the kindest letter from Helen A. Olson, in Devil's Lake, North Dakota. She reads *Plains Folk* in the *Devil's Lake Journal* and says she likes it. What she likes about it, I gather, is that it expresses the spirit of the plains.

Ms. Olson is 86 years old and says, "I got a BA degree from Concordia College in 1929 so I'm an antique." I'm sure she means that the date, not the degree, confers antiquity!

Anyway, she goes on–"I am a native of N.D. and after a lot of traveling in the 49 states and 17 foreign countries, I've really learned what a treasure the vast plains of N.D. are. There's beauty in all four seasons.

"My first trip to New York in 1932 we visited at a home of a 12 year old boy who lived in an apartment. One day he said to me, 'What are plains like?' I explained how we could see for miles over the flat lay of the land.

"He took a deep breath and sighed and said, 'It must be wonderful.'

"I've never forgotten the look on his face. This truly made me appreciate the plains more."

Ms. Olson has another story about the impression made by the plains landscape. She writes, "I had a relative visit from the west coast of Norway where the beautiful fjords are and it is mountainous wherever one looks. I had visited her parents in Norway so I knew of all the beauty there.

"I worried the plains would make her homesick but she soon informed me how wonderful it was to be able to look for miles. To her it was unbelievable and beautiful."

It's been my observation that it is common for people coming from radically different places to be much impressed with the land and people of the plains. When they encounter the country, they do not compare it with home; they can only contrast it, it is so different, and if they are open-minded, they take the country on its own terms.

But the cities of the plains border–Lawrence, Kansas, say, or Fargo, North Dakota–are full of people who hold the level land to the west in contempt. (Except upland game hunters, who hit the trail west regularly.) It seems to be the ambition of every Fargoan to have a cabin in Minnesota. (An old joke: On summer weekends, when so many North

Dakotans head for lake cabins in Minnesota, the average IQ
of both states goes up.)

Unfortunately, the great universities of the plains states
are situated on the regional border. This makes it hard to get
intelligent comment on the problems and opportunities of
plains life out of the universities. On the other hand, I feel
as though I have to go into the heart of the plains frequently
for renewal–to get things into scale, to hear speech of
appropriate cadence, to air out.

Come to think of it, when my mother first came up
from Kansas to visit the Red River valley, she said the
country laid real good.

Most people who achieve any sort of fame by writing
about the plains do so from a distance. Some have just
passed through; their writings are travel narratives. Francis
Parkman (*Oregon Trail*) was the best of these, and Ian
Frazier (*Great Plains*) is a recent example. Others are
children of the land who have gone away from it, but can't
seem to leave it behind. Nebraska's Willa Cather was like
that, and so is North Dakota's Louise Erdrich today.

Kathleen Norris is different. She had spent part of her
childhood in Lemmon, South Dakota, a town of a couple
thousand folks west of the Missouri and just south of the
North Dakota line. About twenty years ago she came
home to Lemmon and took over managing the family farm
interests. She lives there.

People who live in such towns anywhere on the plains
should read Kathleen's book, *Dakota: A Spiritual Geography*.
Even though you might not like everything in it. It's sort of
a holy book. Holy books aren't supposed to make you feel
better, they're supposed to make you be better.

One problem with writing about your hometown is that you have to live with those people. As Kathleen notes, every entry in every minute book of every club concludes with the litany, "A delicious lunch was served." In one chapter heading she asks, "Can You Tell the Truth in a Small Town?"

She does. One chapter, "Gatsby on the Plains," is particularly hard. Kathleen recounts a conversation with a woman who graduated from high school in about 1964 and who thinks that it doesn't get any better than that—"that's what we have to get back to." In times of crisis people like this, instead of doing something constructive, spend their energy laying blame. Parishioners get worked up and fire the minister. Businessmen and bankers turn against farmers in trouble, insisting that they got into trouble through their own mismanagement. Meanwhile, the pulpit goes vacant, and the drugstore closes.

I don't want to give the impression that *Dakota* is a depressing or bitter book. In fact, it's full of affection and beauty. Many passages overflow with a lyric love of level landscapes. Kathleen's account of her experience as substitute pastor of a country congregation shows us what neighborliness should mean. She even finds redeeming social value in that bane of small-town life, gossip. "Gossip" is linguistically close to "gospel" and can be constructive. "Gossip," she says, "is theology translated into experience."

I said before that this is a holy book. Kathleen tells the story of her own faith—how after coming home to Dakota, she worked through her youthful rebellion against religion, made peace with the memory of her grandmothers, and fashioned a new faith whereby a modern woman could re-enter communion with a traditional church.

Protestant herself, she sees life on the plains as something like monastic asceticism, the spare life of the desert fathers. I don't feel quite that way about it, but then, the plains are a different experience for different people.

So named because it lies on the "east end" of the Cypress Hills, Eastend, Saskatchewan, a town of several hundred souls, has a few things going for it. It has the buff-brick Cypress Hotel, still anchoring the main intersection after more than eighty years. It has Jack's Cafe, run by the same Greek family since 1920 (with a picture of the Parthenon above the counter right next to the deer's head and the poster of a sharptail grouse). It has a Tyrannosaurus rex dug up nearby that will become the centerpiece for a new provincial dinosaur museum. It has a beautiful setting in the Frenchman River valley.

Red brick school attended by Wallace Stegner in Eastend, Saskatchewan.

And Eastend has way more than its share of literary life. Eastend, you see, was the boyhood home of Wallace Stegner, dean of Western American writers, Pulitzer prize-winner himself and teacher of Pulitzer prize-winner Larry McMurtry.

Stegner came from a family with shallow roots and lived many places. His parents met and married and lived a few years in Grand Forks, North Dakota, where his father, Fats Stegner, ran a blind pig. After that they moved a lot, ending up in Utah, but during the years 1914-1920 they wintered in Eastend and summered on a Canadian homestead the southern property line of which was the Montana border.

"I may not know who I am," Stegner once wrote, "but I know where I came from," and that place was Eastend– which he calls "Whitemud" in his boyhood memoir, *Wolf Willow*.

It was our good fortune that when my wife and I visited Eastend, the wolf willow was in bloom, flooding the Frenchman valley with the scent that, Stegner says, brought him home again. It also was our good fortune to be hosted in the locality by Peter and Sharon Butala.

Peter, like many a rider before him, is going out in the knees and hips, and so he's easing out of ranching. He and Sharon have deeded the ranch to the Nature Conservancy (an action that has roused quite a bit of local comment pro and con) and are living on what was their hay farm. Sharon is one of Canada's leading novelists and author of a best-selling autobiography, *The Perfection of the Morning*. Like Stegner's, Sharon's books are full of nature and the senses. Must be something in the water around Eastend.

This was a literary pilgrimage for Lotte and me. We have done the Willa Cather tour of Red Cloud; visited the Sandoz sisters in sandhill Nebraska; and located the boyhood home of John Ise in western Kansas. The past couple of years I had been leading discussions of *Wolf Willow* in libraries across North Dakota, and so it was time for us to go to Stegner's roots.

It was worth the trip. The Stegner home is well-preserved by the local arts council and is used as a residence for visiting writers. Down the river are the swimming hole and foot-bridge that figure so prominently in Stegner's recollections. A couple of blocks east is the brick school young Wallace attended and complained of. The Z-X Ranch house (called "Lazy S" in the book) still stands, and Eastenders still haul their trash to the same dump-coulee Stegner remembered as his first lesson in history. Cottonwoods now amply shade the treeless avenues of his youth. The town has named a prominent nearby peak "Jones Peak" after Stegner's local mentor, Corky Jones.

I gather that Stegner, so revered in American letters, is not that well known across Canada. Local and provincial tourist literature barely mention him. American readers, though, are going to find their way to Eastend.

I find myself going back to Eastend, or Whitemud, again and again in my mind, for to me Stegner represents the plains in a way Norris cannot. It's a matter of the senses. I can't get into that ascetic stuff. I want the dust and chaff of a harvest, the cackle of a rising ringneck, the spectacle of a flaming tallgrass prairie, the conviviality of a snow-bound bar and grill—the smell of wolf willow. I want the true plains.

3. Hungry for History

The bluff-top site in Fort Pierre commands an expansive view of the Missouri River valley. You can look across from the Verendrye monument toward Pierre and the earth-sheltered South Dakota Cultural Heritage Center. In that center reposes a piece of lead found on the bluff, near the monument site. This is the Verendrye tablet, and it has a story.

One Sunday in February 1913 some school kids were playing on the Fort Pierre bluffs and found the rectangular lead tablet, about six by eight inches and 3/16-inch thick. There was some strange writing on it, which attracted the interest of one of the kids' fathers and of two state representatives who happened to be hiking in the area. They brought the tablet to the attention of state historian Doane Robinson, who purchased it for his museum.

Robinson recognized that in his hands was the most important piece of metal ever picked up on the plains. On one side is a Latin inscription in block letters; it says that the tablet was placed by Pierre Gaultier de la Verendrye in the twenty-sixth year of King Louis XIV of France, which would have been 1741.

That's not quite true. The tablet was placed in 1743, and by Verendrye's sons, Francois and Louis-Joseph. So on the flip side they scrawled a correction, in French, saying that they, along with a companion, A. Miotte, were responsible. According to their journal, they put the tablet under a stone cairn.

Their journal does not amount to much. In it the
French explorers give a rough narrative of their expedition,
but you cannot reconstruct from it where they did what.
That's why finding the tablet was so important. It places
the explorers at the moment they built that cairn and
buried the tablet. We know thereby that in 1742-43 the
brothers Verendrye, exploring from French Canada in a
frustrating and futile search for the western sea, came south-
west across North Dakota and South Dakota as far as the
Black Hills, then returned north and east across the middle
of the Dakotas.

This is historic, but more interesting to me is what we
make of things like this Verendrye tablet. I have observed
that people on the plains are hungry for history. They long
to own a piece of it.
That's why, judging
from the monu-
ments erected by
enthusiastic citi-
zens, Fray Juan de
Padilla of the
Coronado expedi-
tion died four times,
and why, the pro-
tests of the state

Ralph's Ruts sign on Highway 56, staking a
claim to History in Rice County, Kansas.

highway department notwithstanding, Ralph Hathaway,
one of my old neighbors in western Kansas, keeps putting
up those signs proclaiming the way to Ralph's Ruts on the
old Santa Fe Trail. This is good. It's a sign of something,
I'm not sure what, but something good.

Now back to Fort Pierre. Naturally, people here claim
possession of the Verendryes by virtue of having the tablet.

There were skeptics in other states who said the tablet might have been carried from elsewhere to the Fort Pierre site by Indians, that the tablet is no proof the Verendryes ever stood where I stood on that bluff overlooking the Missouri.

Part of me takes this with the same skepticism I hold toward all those people on the southern plains who insist that Coronado traipsed across their farms because they plowed up pieces of chain mail. But when you get up close to that tablet in the Heritage Center, it feels better to believe.

Besides, if I don't believe their stories, they might not believe mine.

When in 1913 those kids found the Verendrye tablet on a bluff in Fort Pierre, it was an important day for historians. The tablet was not just a 170-year-old curiosity. It was the key piece to a puzzle, allowing scholars to reconstruct the route of the French explorers' journey of exploration across the plains in 1742-43.

But what did it mean to the children who uncovered this sensational artifact? Not much at the time, but once the public fuss began, it meant a great deal. It's interesting to read the clippings and letters in the files of the South Dakota State Historical Society whereby various parties put forward and disputed their claims to have found or been in some way involved with finding the tablet.

George O'Rielly was the first. He said he and other boys, brandishing wooden swords, were playing battle on the Fort Pierre bluffs and found the tablet while digging a trench. This contradicted the story of a girl named Ethel Parrish (later Hepner) who said that she and another girl,

Hattie Foster, were with George that day, and that Hattie
found the tablet by tripping over it. After George cleaned
the dirt off with his pocket knife, she said, the three of them
agreed that he would try to sell the lead tablet for scrap.

George revised his story to include the girls, but he grew
irked over the years with accounts that cast him as a rascal
and bully. Some said that after Hattie found the tablet, he
snatched it from her and ran away with it. As an adult,
George would say, "That's a lot of bunk."

Then too, Hattie later tried to claim that her sister
Blanche also was there. Ethel protested this rank revision-
ism. Eventually, however, an official publication of the
state historical society would name seven kids who were
there, and Blanche made the list.

There seems to have been some gender conflict going
on here. George, the boy, considered himself the discov-
erer of record, even though Hattie had picked up the tablet
first. Indeed, state museum ledgers disclose that George
and his father collected the $200 appropriated by the
South Dakota legislature to buy the artifact.

Two legislators were involved with the discovery
because they happened to meet George and his father at
the Fort Pierre depot. The two politicians, of course, later
would recall that they played important roles. Representative Elmer Anderson said it was he who called in state
historian Doane Robinson, thereby seeing that the state
acquired the leaden treasure.

According to Representative G.W. White, though, he
knew the story of the Verendryes, recognized the tablet
immediately, felt "an indescribable feeling" from head to
foot when he touched it, translated the Latin inscription
himself, and called Robinson about it.

Who owns history, anyway? Well, Ethel Parrish Hepner outlived all the rest of them, and so the last published word, in 1989, was hers. But it doesn't much matter who found the Verendrye tablet, or who was there when it happened. The point is that this piece of lead is important enough to argue about. It makes Fort Pierre, South Dakota, a place of antiquity.

After composing a couple of columns about the famous Verendrye tablet—on permanent and prominent exhibit in the South Dakota Cultural Heritage Center—I thought I had pretty well finished with this story.

Not so, it seems, for in 1995 my friends in South Dakota told me that another Verendrye plate had been discovered. This was sensational.

It seems a fellow named Max Rittgers—an expatriate South Dakotan living in Florida—decided to make a float trip down the Cheyenne River, in West River South Dakota. It was said that after suffering several family misfortunes, he was seeking solace in outdoor adventure. He was accompanied by his three-year-old Labrador retriever, Ben.

Rittgers said that during this trip, on 4 May 1995, Ben found something on a hillside, marked it (as retrievers are inclined to do), and then stayed on the spot, waiting for Rittgers to come see what he had found. Lassie-like.

Just a corner of metal protruded from the ground, but when freed from the earth, it proved to be a plate of lead about six by seven inches. Rittgers didn't think much about it, until water washed off the dirt and revealed a scratched inscription: "A. Miotte Le 7 de Marse 1743."

The Verendrye tablet in Pierre has a Latin inscription on one side, and on the other, a note including the names

of the Verendryes and of this other chap, A. Miotte. This
new find didn't have the Latin side, just the scratchings in
French. Hmmm.

Historians and curators in the region were greatly
interested. Dates and places in the story seemed to match up
with the narrative of the Verendrye expedition. Said
Rittgers, "A fellow who has studied the Verendrye expeditions all of his life held the plate and his hands trembled."

Rittgers began speaking publicly about the find and
sending photos of it to museums. He said a private collector
offered him a million dollars, but he didn't want money. He
just wanted the tablet to go to an appropriate museum, and–
he wanted Ben to get credit for the discovery.

All this struck me as admirable at first, especially the dog
part. Then I started studying the news clippings kindly
provided me by friends in the State Historical Society of
South Dakota.

In the first place, Rittgers seemed to have a defensive
attitude toward those who were skeptical of or just not
sufficiently interested in his story. Second, he seemed in no
great hurry to have the tablet authenticated by metallur-
gists or handwriting experts. Third, officials of the Bureau
of Land Management noticed that according to Rittgers's
story, the tablet was found on public land. There are laws
against removing antiquities from federal lands.

Then came the capper. Rittgers hired an airplane and
pilot, flew out over the West River, and tossed the tablet
into the Cheyenne–along with three other packages, to
confuse anyone watching and trying to retrieve the artifact. "The river reclaimed its history with a splash," he
wrote. So we'll never get expert opinion on the artifact

The author with Bancroft, the History Dog. If you know retrievers, then you know what to think of Max Rittgers's story of the Verendrye tablet.

itself. I don't think we need it, however.

This story doesn't wash. The dog element is the problem. A three-year-old Labrador retriever, to begin with, is dumb as a stump. More to the point, such a beast is not interested in little metal objects partially buried in the ground. If it was a pork chop, or a dead frog, yes. A lead plate, no. A three-year-old Labrador retriever would not even notice the object if he stepped on it, and he most certainly would not linger over it and summon his master.

I would say, if this fellow Rittgers offers to sell you a lead tablet, offer him a three-dollar bill for it.

4. Winter Survival Kit

On 12 January 1888 a terrific blizzard hit central Nebraska. Horror tales of this visitation abound, and several deal with teachers and pupils at isolated country schools. There was teacher Loie Royce of Plainfield, who tried to make it home with three of her pupils, but all three perished in the drifts, and she suffered the loss of both feet. And there was poor Etta Shattuck, who sent her children home, then herself became lost, spent three days in a haystack, and died shortly afterward.

Then there was Minnie Freeman, heroine of Mira Valley, right in the middle of the sandhills. The blizzard blew in the door of her sod schoolhouse, and then off came part of the roof. Miss Freeman got the children together and knotted them into a line, using a ball of twine she had taken away from one who had been playing with it during class. Then, carrying the youngest, she coaxed them along to a farmhouse, three-quarters of a mile away, into the wind.

The national wire services played these little schoolhouse dramas for all they were worth, and suddenly Minnie Freeman was known across the land. A Mrs. Ellis of St. Paul, Nebraska, wrote a poem about her. A fellow in San Francisco, California, sent her a gold watch inscribed to commemorate "her heroism in saving the lives of thirteen pupils during the storm of January 12, 1888." Set into the back of the case were thirteen rubies—one for each child.

Finally, one William Vincent published the parlor song, "Thirteen Were Saved," or, "Nebraska's Fearless Maid." I am indebted to Paul Haack of the University of Kansas for sending me the sheet music and to the folks at the Nebraska State Historical Society for providing background information.

"Thirteen Were Saved"–what a hokey song it is. Loosely based on a wire service interview with Miss Freeman, it embellishes the tale considerably and packs it with the sort of sentimentality contrived to wring tears from a hedge post. Miss Freeman, on the other hand, was quite matter-of-fact about what she had done.

Still, I pass this song out for some of my history classes to study, because the song tells us just what people expected of the country schoolteacher in the late nineteenth century. We learn from it nothing about whether she taught anyone to read or write or cipher. What was more important was that she kept order in the classroom. She caught Frankie Gibbon playing with that ball of twine, and she took it away from him.

She also, as the song says, was "a plucky little maid." The country schoolteacher was to be unmarried, and although assertiveness might be frowned upon, pluck was a virtue. After all, there might not always be a man around to get her out of trouble.

Most important, at three points in a three-stanza song, Miss Freeman or someone else involved calls on God for help. The teacher was to be a moral example.

Minnie Freeman three years later married a man named Edgar B. Penny; lived some years in Fullerton, Nebraska; moved to Chicago, Illinois; and died there in 1943, at the age of seventy-five.

Minnie Freeman's virtue, courage, and clear thinking saved her class during the great Nebraska blizzard of 1888. Blizzard stories are standard fare up and down the plains, and many of them have to do with pupils at risk between home and school. Some, like the story of Minnie Freeman, conclude triumphantly. Others, like that of Hazel Miner, turn tragic.

Sixteen-year-old Hazel; her brother Emmett, age eleven; and sister Myrdith, age nine, in 1920 were attending Center Consolidated School, in the middle of North Dakota. This is along present State Highway 25, northwest of Bismarck. Local historian Lucille Gullickson says that this exposed stretch of highway, which follows a divide through the hills, is known to residents as a "blizzard belt."

I found the old Center Consolidated School now serving as a family residence. Pearl Rhone welcomed me into her family home, showed me the remodeling that had been done, pointed out the window toward the old school barn, and took down from the wall a framed newspaper account of the death of Hazel Miner.

By mid-March 1920 North Dakota had seen some warm weather, melting most of the winter's accumulation of snow, filling the coulees with run-off. On 15-16 March, however, blizzard conditions descended, with heavy snows flying before winds exceeding forty miles per hour.

Tuesday, 16 March, the Miner children were in school. William Miner, their father, concerned for their safety coming home, rode his saddle horse to the school. He intended to lead the children home with the horse and sleigh they had taken in the morning. He hitched up the

sleigh, put the children in, and walked away to get his
saddle horse. The horse hitched to the sleigh suddenly
dashed off into the blizzard, and the sleigh was lost from
sight immediately.

William Miner rode home, and finding his children not
there, got neighbors out to search. The next day they found
the sleigh and children a little more than a mile east of the
school. The Miner home was a mile directly north of the
school.

The younger Miner children later recounted what had
happened. After the initial runaway, the horse slowed and
halted, but they were disoriented and could not see where
they were going. The tugs came loose, and Hazel got out of
the sleigh to re-hitch, getting wet to the waist. She led the
horse for a while. Then
Emmett led, and the sleigh,
after descending the gentle
slope of a coulee, over-
turned in the gully at the
bottom. The children were
unable to right it.

They took cover on the
lee side of the overturned
sleigh and tried to fashion a
shelter with their lap robe,
but it kept blowing loose,
and they kept getting
colder. Finally Hazel told
the two younger children
to lie down, spread the
robe over them, and then

Memorial to heroic Hazel Miner,
Center, North Dakota.

lay atop it. The searchers next day found them that way–the children below safe, Hazel frozen to death.

Lucille Gullickson's husband, Elmer, took me out to the spot where Hazel Miner perished. It was less than a half-mile from a farmhouse.

The Miner family must have been poor. There is no marker on Hazel's grave. In 1936 Governor L.B. Hanna dedicated a stone memorial by the courthouse in Center. Folksinger Chuck Suchy has recorded a ballad commemorating Hazel Miner's heroism. And she has a living memorial in that North Dakotans have incorporated her story into their cultural mythology of a hardy people battling a hostile environment.

It seems somehow significant that whereas Nebraska's blizzard heroine lives on triumphant, North Dakota's Hazel Miner, just as virtuous, dies a martyr to the implacable elements.

I remember the first time, after going to work for North Dakota State University, I picked up a state car to take on a business trip. I opened up the trunk to load my gear and found there was no room for it. The trunk was just about filled by a big wooden box labeled, "Winter Survival Kit."

I hope inside there is a Dakota Heat survival candle. This little item was the idea of a farmer-turned-gas station operator named Lyle Milbrandt, in Lisbon, North Dakota, in the early 1960s. Milbrandt, considering the usual advice given to winter travelers of the northern plains that they should carry candles in their cars, decided that wasn't enough. He designed a paraffin-filled pan with multiple wicks designed to burn for many hours and generate plenty of heat. He called this the "Mytee Glo," produced it for a few years in a shop in Lisbon, and then sold the product name to a firm in South Dakota.

The business revived in 1978 when the Southwestern Bus Company of Minnesota contacted another businessman in Lisbon, Morrie Saxerud, with the proposition he manufacture 20,000 survival candles. These were not just for the buses. One son of the owner of the bus company, a graduate of Brigham Young University, believed there would be a powerful market for the candles among members of the Church of Jesus Christ of the Latter Day Saints; the Mormons, he thought, would want the candles to include with their family caches of food and emergency supplies.

The Mormon market never firmed up, but Saxerud, with an inventory on his hands, started selling to the general public. He has been producing what he calls the Dakota Heat candle ever since. (This is a side line for his firm, which mainly does assembly for a larger manufacturer.)

The Dakota Heat is, in fact, an 8x8 brownie pan filled with paraffin. A screen circle encloses a pure paraffin ring, sporting twelve wicks, in the middle of the pan; the corners are filled with insulation material.

Dakota Heat candle, manufactured in Lisbon, North Dakota.

Saxerud's three sons financed college by making Dakota Heat candles. Now he hires a few high school or college

students to produce some 4000 over the summer months.
They set up the pans, insert the wicks into screens to hold
them up, and pour the melted paraffin from sprinkler cans–
all hand labor. Saxerud sells them to hardware and sporting
goods stores. The state of South Dakota equips all state
vehicles with Dakota Heat candles.

The Dakota Heat candle is proven to burn for 24 hours.
I figured there must be a lot of great stories from customers
who got stranded in blizzards and survived terrible ordeals by
lighting up their Dakota Heat candles. In fact, only one
customer has ever told Saxerud he made use of one of his
candles, but he reported it worked fine. "He said the only
problem was that it smoked up the car," relates the manufacturer, "and he didn't mind that a bit."

I still don't know if there's a Dakota Heat candle in that
mysterious box in my North Dakota state car. God willing,
I'll never find out.

5. Und Auch der Belzenickel

At the Lawrence Welk homestead—you have to have a nylon jacket with something on the back of it.

What I kept thinking, as I moved through the sunny Sunday-afternoon crowds attending the dedication of the Welk homestead just north of Strasburg, North Dakota, is that I've got to get one of those jackets. A nylon jacket that says "Grafton Curling Club," or "South Dakota Hunter Safety Program," or "North Dakota Centennial 1889-1989," or something, on the back.

The site was the family farm of Ludwig and Christina Welk, Black-Sea German-Russian immigrants, the parents of Lawrence Welk, America's music maker. His autobiography, *Wunnerful, Wunnerful*, sold ten million copies. His television show, now syndicated by the Oklahoma Public Television Authority, is the most popular show on public television nation-wide.

Most people have an image of Lawrence Welk. (Mine comes from having to watch him at my grandparents' house. I'm gratified my daughter informs me that her grandmother has made her watch Lawrence Welk, too, "as a cultural experience," she says.) But there is a lot more to the Lawrence Welk story than accordions, polkas, and the champagne of bottled beer. My trip to Strasburg gave me a glimpse of the rest of the story—the homely, ethnic roots of the Welk success story.

There was a parade in town in the morning. Unfortunately, there were no bands in the parade, but there was a neat float by the German-Russian society, proclaiming, "Arbeit macht das Leben suss." ("Work is what makes life sweet.")

Then everyone got into cars to drive three miles to the homestead. Cars backed up for two miles. People got out on the road and walked across the fields, leaving one person to bring the car along. ("If I don't get there, honey, take lots of pictures.") It was like a festive funeral procession. Coincidentally, Lawrence Welk had died in California two weeks before.

There were a couple of undercurrents of discontent. Some German-Russians in the locality still resent it that Lawrence never announced his ethnic roots. This is understandable, I think. He began his television career in the middle of the Red Scare, and the folks at Miller Brewing probably wouldn't have appreciated Lawrence announcing his Russian parentage to the world. Then there was the incident during Saturday night mass at St. Peter and Paul Church, a stunningly beautiful structure. The Welk descendants were there for a family reunion, and the priest, in his sermon, made some rambling remarks about wealthy people who fail to share their fortunes with their old friends and neighbors.

None of this surfaced at the homestead celebration, however. Dignitaries expounded, T-shirts were sold, a local band (including an ambidextrous fellow who played drums and trumpet at the same time) played, people milled around, the barn swallows panicked and streaked around madly. Older ladies kept coming up to me and saying, "When's Myron Floren going to play?" He finally did, and Norma Zimmer, the Champagne Lady, danced with local folk.

The more interesting things were off-stage, in the throng. No tourists around–these were all Dakota plains folk. The nylon jackets, the headwear (among males, some 70 percent caps, all bearing some sort of legend, and some 30 percent cowboy hats), the groups of widows who had come together, the old guys passing around bags of sunflower seeds. And the faces–such faces– faces that looked like relief maps, marked by ages of erosion. Everyday faces I will not forget.

Dakota faces at the Lawrence Welk homestead dedication, Strasburg.

Months later I took a tour group out to Strasburg. Although we went to the Welk homestead, there was more to explore than the origins of the renowned entertainer. We were looking into German-Russian culture–of the Black Sea Catholic German variety, not Mennonite or Volga German, such as I knew in Kansas.

Near the little town of Hague we walked around a country cemetery filled with iron-cross grave markers crafted by local smiths. These are sublime pieces of folk art, but some of the things happening around the old Hague cemetery are unsettling. Someone has spray-painted all the crosses silver. That's all wrong; they need to be black. I think.

Worse, someone has planted seedling trees in rows on both sides of the cemetery. I suppose the intent is to make things more pleasant for tourists stopping by, but that's all wrong, too. Trees don't belong in a Black Sea German cemetery. These are plains folk resting here.

What most impressed my group, though, was the beautiful St. Peter and Paul Church of Strasburg. Father Leonard Eckroth was cordial, and the ladies of the German-Russian Heritage Society served coffee and kuchen in the basement. But it was the ornamentation of the church, even more than the hospitality of its parishioners, that was stunning.

As you enter, you are likely to overlook the Pieta to your left, because your eyes are drawn into the beautiful sanctuary. The statuary, painstakingly restored, the wealth of stained glass, and the vaulted ceilings inspire awe. You think, all this, in the little town of Strasburg.

Then you are inclined to think that the folk responsible for this must have been lions of the church–not only pioneers of the plains, but also perpetuators of the faith, worthy of veneration. St. Fidelis Church of Victoria, Kansas (the so-called Cathedral of the Plains), inspires the same sort of awe (although I think I prefer the church in Pfeifer, with its alcove of stained-glass windows depicting the settlement of western Kansas).

These pioneers, although they erected great monuments to their faith, had their human foibles. They could be downright ornery at times. I know this from reading the memoir of Father Justus Schweizer, who filled the pulpit at Strasburg for a few years just after 1900 (before the big church was built in 1909-11). Father Justus's writings were recently discovered in the archives of an abbey in Einsiedeln, Switzerland.

Even before the good father arrived in Strasburg, the parish priest in Aberdeen, South Dakota, had advised him, "I know these German-Russians. They are great people with much good but are also intermixed with some bad self-determination." He called them "Kopekenspalter," which is to say, penny-pinchers.

Later Father Justus's bishop would say, "These German-Russians are the biggest burden in my diocese. They have their scrapes with their priests in almost every parish."

The priest did have his scrapes with the folk at Strasburg, beginning with his first mass. He quizzed the young folk of the congregation on their catechismical knowledge and found them wanting. (Asked, "What is marriage?", a young woman replied, "The place where sins of an earlier life are burned away.")

Father Justus insisted the people should establish a parish school. They fought him all the way and also re-mained fond of drinking and dancing.

Somehow, these same folks, within five years, would erect St. Peter and Paul Church. Go figure.

"Darf's Christkindl hereinkommen?" At the door of a farmhouse in McHenry County, North Dakota, stood a woman dressed in white finery, her face veiled. Invited, she came in, asking, "Und auch der Belzenickel?" Whereupon a scowling man in a fur coat, carrying a chain, followed her into the room.

The Christkindl, the gentle woman in white, wanted to hear your prayers. If you didn't know them, or if you had been bad children, well, then you had the Belzenickel to deal with.

What Terry Wald remembers about the Christkindl and the Belzenickel is not unusual. Her memories are important, rather, because they are so common. In German-Russian communities across the plains, from Kansas to Saskatchewan, every Christmas season the Christkindl and the Belzenickel made the rounds.

We visited with Terry in her home in Grand Forks and asked what else she remembered about them. She recounts her first recollection: "I think Mr. Mossier was it [the Belzenickel] that year. But I was not preoccupied with him, because his daughter Frances was the Christkindl, and she smelled so nice."

The Belzenickel did not come every year of her childhood, Terry says, "but we were threatened with him every year." Somehow the Belzenickel knew about whatever mischief you had been up to, and he was fearsome enough to put the fear of God into any troublesome child. "The mothers had control of how much fright could be put into their children," Terry concludes.

"Christkindl" means "Christ-child." It's a mystery how Christ came to be represented by a woman in this custom. "Belzenickel" comes from "Pelz-Saint Nicklaus," or a Saint Nicklaus wearing fur. These figures go back to Russia and before that to Germany.

My wife Lotte, a German citizen, recalls when the Belzenickel came to her house, stuffed her into a sack, and carried her off. That was a year she had caused her mother a lot of trouble, she says. (That could have been any year, I say.)

The custom of the Christkindl and the Belzenickel seems to have died out, except where someone deliberately decides to reenact it. That's what Terry and her (late) husband, Ben, did one year in the early 1980s, when they were living in Minot.

She bought an old wedding gown at the Salvation Army for three dollars, and she fashioned a crown from garland. Ben got out an old horse-blanket, into which Terry sewed a new red lining. And out they went to visit older family and friends.

First there were Uncle Joe and Aunt Anna Wald, who, on the unexpected appearance of the Christkindl and the Belzenickel, seemed transported. "You're really her, aren't you?", Aunt Anna mused. Visiting other relatives, Ben, who was in poor health, tired, and so Mary Streifel Wood took over the role of the Belzenickel.

Donning the horse-blanket, she remarked to Ben that somehow she had never seen the Belzenickel, but only heard him outside. Don't you know, he replied–your father **was** the Belzenickel!

I wonder if this Christmas season, somewhere on these plains, the Christkindl is knocking?

6. Something Odd in Absaraka

These college girls who had been studying in the library one evening decided to go back to the dorm and turn in. They walked over in a group and accompanied one of their number to her room, which was darkened as they entered. "Don't turn on the light," she cautioned. "I don't want to wake up my roommate." The others left, and the girl slipped into bed and fell asleep.

Next morning she woke to find her roommate horribly murdered. Written in red on the bathroom mirror was the legend, "Aren't you glad you didn't turn on the light?"

What you have just read is an example of a modern American legend. Folklore isn't dead in our society; it just takes strange forms.

This particular story is found across the country–including among students at North Dakota State University. I pick these things up from my classes.

A scholar named Jan Brunvand has made a career collecting and studying these stories, which he calls "urban legends." They're legends, all right, but I'm dubious about the "urban" part. I find that they flourish across rural America, too.

Some of these legends are famous as teenage scare stories. I mean ones like "The Vanishing Hitch-hiker," "The Choking Doberman," and of course, "The Bloody Hook."

The old ones keep coming back into circulation, while new ones come into currency. For instance, there's that story that turned up last year about the woman whose brains were leaking out.

This fellow came out of the grocery store on a hot afternoon, see, and in the parking lot he noticed a woman sitting in her car, head on the steering wheel. He knocked on the window and, when she failed to move, opened the door.

"Call an ambulance," the woman moaned. "I've been shot in the back of the head and my brain is leaking out."

The guy ran inside and called for emergency services, then returned to the stricken woman. He asked her how she had come to be shot.

"I don't know," she said. "I put my groceries in the back seat, and as I was getting ready to start the car I heard the shot and felt the bullet. I reached back and felt my brains leaking out."

The police arrived and discovered that there had been a can of refrigerated bread dough in the woman's groceries; it had exploded and struck her in the back of the head; and the dough stuck there felt to her like brains.

Could have happened, right?

"A few friends and I heard a rumor," one of my students told me, "about something odd in the town of Absaraka. We had heard that strange things were going on in the old abandoned Methodist church. So, ten of us went to the site, not too far away from where we live."

Let me interject right here that it is heartening to see young people taking care of this type of business. Traditionally, it is the duty of teenagers to investigate these sorts of community problems, determine the facts, and embroider them suitably. Now back to the story.

"We walked up to the church to find many lights around it, and a big NO TRESPASSING sign on the side of the church. We also noticed that many of the windows were boarded up." One was not fully covered, however, and so they peered inside.

"Then we focused inside the dark void, and to our astonishment, we saw a gigantic glowing cross! We knew that it was inside, because we could not see all of it, and it moved in the window when we would move from side to side, as if it was inside the church. People that have made it inside in the daylight tell us there is nothing inside the church except for dust and cobwebs."

Then there was the young woman who recalled a sad incident back home in Aberdeen, South Dakota. Submitted for your examination: "In our arena we have catwalks above the gym floor where janitors walk and make sure everything is OK. In the 1960s during one of our 'Pop, Popcorn, and Pops' choir concerts, a janitor was up on the catwalks throwing balloons down on the audience. Well, he fell off and died.

"Now people say that his ghost still lives in the arena. He has his own chair, it is something like section 0, row C, seat 13. The high school is Aberdeen Central High."

Legends of the plains–there's no end to them. A legend is a type of story, a folk narrative. It is told for true, and may well be; it is told for entertainment, although it may have some deeper meaning; and it usually contains some element of the fantastic. But it need not dwell on matters paranormal.

For instance, another student of mine recalled a memorable Thanksgiving meal at his grandmother's house. After the turkey and trimmings had been consumed, it was time for dessert. "My grandma had prepared three kinds of pie," he recounted. "I chose chocolate. This would be one of the greatest mistakes of my life."

The grandmother asked if anyone wanted whipped cream and brought out "a massive tub of Cool Whip. Upon opening the Cool Whip, the top is covered with mold. I swear the whole top was green.

"Grandma grabs the spoon sitting next to me and stirs up the Cool Whip so the mold is no longer visible. I sit in shock as she whips the biggest dollop of Cool Whip I had ever seen in my life onto my plate.

"Anyway she threw the Cool Whip on a couple of other people's pies, too, and all of us were too shy (or stupid) to say something. I was proud of my intestinal fortitude keeping it down.

"My grandma still has the same tub of Cool Whip in her fridge and a bottle of BBQ sauce that expired before I was born."

I think I might be related to this guy.

Absaraka United Methodist church, home of the glowing cross.

Painted yellow by the September sunlight, Absaraka in the afternoon has nothing paranormal about it. Take the blacktop jogging north and west from I-94 through Wheatland and follow it west, through fields of nodding sunflowers and beans, to where it crosses the Burlington railway. On your right as you enter town is Absaraka United Methodist Church.

Somehow this white, wood-frame, cross-gabled former house of worship became a destination for teen-age pilgrims from Casselton and towns around here, as well as from the city, Fargo. I learned about this from an NDSU student who reported there was "something odd in Absaraka," something having to do with the Methodist church. My informants from surrounding towns confirm that this got to be a regular routine with high-school kids, some of whom even forced their way inside the abandoned church. Local folk disliked the disturbance, and sheriff's deputies got tired of coming out. What was taking place was an example of what folklorists call a "teen-age legend trip."

All this explains the ambiguity of signage around the church. The sign out front still says, "Absaraka United Methodist Church–Welcome!" But a little sign tacked to the corner of the building says, "No Trespassing–Violators Will Be Prosecuted." Another stuck in the ground indicates, "Private Drive." Turquoise-painted plywood covers all windows, and a padlock and chain drape the front door.

Here comes the village blacksmith, bicycling toward his shop, Minnesota Vikings on his forehead. He lives next door to the church, and that's his shop, clad in stamped tin, on the south side of the street. It stands across from the post office (58002), a white-frame, false-fronted building that used to house the general store. "It was a heck of a store–you could buy anything there," says the smith. "I miss that place."

Just this side of the smithy is Absaraka Centennial Park, a little plaza of memorials noting Chester Thompson's plat of the town in 1881 and a roster of designated "pioneers."

"Absaraka," I learn, means "home of the crows." The place of honor, the plaque on the flagpole, goes to John Faught "for many years of dedication to Little League and amateur baseball." Along with his

False-fronted Absaraka Post Office, the only public building remaining in town.

name and legend, a bat, ball, mitt, and cap are engraved on the plaque. To the south, abutting the railway, is a well-kept ballfield. In fact, overall, for a town without a retail business, Absaraka is remarkably clean and well-maintained.

The smith explains how he thinks the glowing-cross story got started. Back of the church once stood a lamppost, light from which streamed through the back windows and was reflected out the front. There doesn't seem to be any narrative behind the glowing cross, no tragic story, just the image of the cross. It's a sort of postmodern legend-without-a-story.

He says the church now belongs to several members of the Monilaws family, one of whom I got hold of in Valley City. She confirms, "When the windows aren't boarded up, you can see crosses in the windows," and "it just looks really neat." On the other hand, she agrees with the smith's explanation—lamp lights reflected off light fixtures inside onto the frosted window glass. The Monilaws keep the place up, like the rest of the town.

Because of problems with legend-trippers—"It got to be
every week there was damage"—a burglar alarm has been
installed in the church, and the sheriff's office keeps a pretty
good eye on the place. So I wonder where the venturesome
kids are headed tonight?

Investigating the story of the glowing cross in Absaraka
United Methodist Church, I came up with what to me
were some disturbing findings. Judging by previous experience with such things, I figured there must be a story to
explain it, but there isn't. There's just the glowing cross,
and you look at it, and then you go home. This is lame,
I thought.

So next I went out in search of the glowing graves at
Dickey. This I heard about from kids who went to school at
Marion or Lamoure or places nearby. Of nights they
cruised over to Dickey, cut their lights, and pulled up to the
cemetery. And the graves glowed. How come, I said—What's
the story? No story. The graves just glow.

Unbelieving, I went looking for the story. I checked it
out at the Farmer's Cafe, where I was the only customer,
and a woman about my age was peeling apples for a pie.
Oh sure, she'd heard about the glowing graves, but she
hadn't seen them. It was a big deal a few years ago, when
her kids were in high school. One night she had a bunch of
them in the station wagon, and she said, Let's go see the
glowing graves—but the kids were too chicken. What's the
story behind this, I asked. She said there isn't any story.
The graves just glow.

In the Cenex station I found a gathering of the local
literati, story-tellers for sure, four or five of them, and they

confirmed the certain fact that the graves glow. How come, I asked? What's the story? No story.

A Bronco was parked at the church, where the itinerant priest was preparing for the next day's services. What's the story, I asked. He said, the priest would be the last one to know.

If there's no story, then what's the big deal? What makes a teenage legend trip now? In other words, how does folklore work these days?

To find out I drove away from town, put down my notebook and other historical trappings, and then drove back into town, eyes and ears open. Dickey has an unmistakable sense of place. You come in by descending from arrow-straight 46 Highway, exiting north onto county 63 and into the mile-wide, slope-shouldered James River valley. On your right as you approach town is the village cemetery, not the one with the glowing graves, but one sufficient to set a tone. Across it to the north is the pale, stuccoed Assumption Catholic Church.

Right there is the turning point. If you turn east, you enter Wholesome Hometown U.S.A., a compact little main street anchored by a grain elevator on the Red River Valley and Western Railroad. Here are the Farmer's Cafe, the Cenex, the post office, the State Bank of Dickey, the "Biggest Little Town in the World Pop. 74" sign, and around the corner, the necessary Dickey Bar. Nothing paranormal here.

But if you turn west, onto the prairie road, things are different. Just behind you is the village cemetery, the pale church alongside, and across from that a big two-story stucco house with a spooky dormer. In front of you, 3/10 of a

mile west up the prairie road, is the Assumption Catholic
Cemetery, and there are the glowing graves.

Here are about four acres enclosed by web wire, scraggly
elms coming up in the fencerows. A large wooden cross
stands at center, next to a lone spruce tree. Most of the
markers are granite, but there are pale marble tombstones
in a couple of family plot areas. These are glowers. Most
striking, there is a single, unmarked, white-painted grave
cross in the northwest corner. It's home-made, welded in
somebody's shop. I'll bet you can see that one from the
county road on a good night.

No story. But looking around, contemplating the
dreary tree-clad slopes bounding the valley, sitting on that
unidentified, cross-marked grave, I get it. It's the place.

7. Great Plains Grotesque

"Bizarre" is a word that appears in many written descriptions of the place. "Horrible" was the reaction of my spouse to it. I prefer the adjective "grotesque," or better, "Great Plains grotesque," for this creation is surely of the plains. I'm talking about the Petrified Wood Garden, in Lemmon, South Dakota.

The plains of North America have a number of grotesque environments created by visionary individuals. The Garden of Eden, in Lucas, Kansas; Carhenge, at Alliance, Nebraska; and the Valley of the Dinosaurs, at Drumheller, Alberta, are in the same class with Lemmon's Petrified Wood Garden.

Lemmon, a town of 1600 or so, is situated in the beautiful butte country of West River South Dakota. It has attracted some national attention because it is the setting of *Dakota: A Spiritual Geography*, by Kathleen Norris, a Lemmon resident.

Its prior claim to fame, the Petrified Wood Garden, was the creation of Ole S. Quammen, who came into Lemmon on the first passenger train, in 1907, and opened a lumber yard. He prospered economically and became interested scientifically in the petrified wood and many other fossil remains to be found in the Lemmon vicinity. He gathered the stuff, and he and his wheelchair-bound son, David, studied it.

In about 1926 Quammen began work on what was to be the park. He hired a crew of men to gather petrified

wood, hauling it in with teams and with Fords. He hired
another crew, supervised by John Rafferty, for construction,
and over the next few years, astonishing structures arose.
These were hard times, and local cowboys were glad to have
work on Quammen's project.

It covered more than a city block near the junction of
highways 12 and 73. On the northwest corner arose a gas
station built of petrified wood, and behind that some larger
buildings of the same material. All around, Rafferty's crew
constructed cones, or pyramids, a hundred of them, of

petrified wood and
cannonball boul-
ders (round sand-
stones from the
Cannonball River).
Benches, a wishing
well, and other odd
structures added to
the complex.

**Castle in Petrified Wood Park, Lemmon,
South Dakota.**

Most notable
was the castle, 24
feet by 24, 24 feet high, with turrets. Its floor, like the
walkways all around the park, was of petrified grass slabs.

Quammen held a dedication on 7 June 1932. He had
motion pictures taken and barbecued four steers for visitors.
Two years later, both he and his son died, and the park was
inherited by his daughter, Alice Olson. She deeded it to the
city in 1956, and in 1961 the city turned it over to the
Petrified Wood Park Historical Society, operating under the
authority of the city and the Chamber of Commerce. Today
the Chamber office is in the gas station, and a historical

museum in the large outbuilding behind. Twelve thousand
visitors registered in 1992.

Thirty-two hundred tons of petrified wood, and untold
quantities of cannonballs, fossils, and other geological
curiosities–the effect of a twilight walk through this complex
is more than I can describe. I noticed electrical outlets here
and there, and the curator told me that they string lights
from the structures at Christmas. This I had
to see.

Early and heavy snows had laid siege to the West River
country of the northern plains. Herds of deer gnawed dens
into big round bales. Pheasants by the hundred huddled
around farmsteads, foraging for feed in the hog pens and
silage piles. Plows were slow to clear the long highways.

In Lemmon, South Dakota, a few citizens were out in
brown duck coveralls, dragging lights and cords through
the drifts. Move over Winnipeg, self-styled Christmas City
of the Prairies. Give it up, you promoters of Denver's
Larimer Street or Kansas City's Plaza. No one lights for
Christmas like Lemmon.

Because no one else has the Petrified Wood Park, that
fantastic village of petrified wood and cannonball boulders
assembled by Ole Quammen and his hands during the
1920s and 1930s. If you haven't seen it, go first during
summer, when you can walk about the castles and cones in
leisure and comfort.

I knew the park was wired and lighted for Christmas,
and so when an invitation from the folks in Lemmon
arrived, I diverted from a pheasant hunting expedition and
came over for the lighting ceremony.

This started seven years ago with a little committee of
the Chamber of Commerce. I talked with current committee members Tori Kling and Shari Helland, local girls who
had gone away to get degrees and then returned to join an
accounting firm in Lemmon. Now they're stuck, because
once people get suckered into the lighting committee,
"They don't get off unless they die," Tori says.

There are at least 400 strings of lights used, many of the
one-goes-out-and-they-all-go-out variety. Committee
members and volunteers turn out for several nights the last
week of October to check lights. The first Saturday of
November they string the cords and lights and erect the
nativity scene built by the FFA boys, but there is always
follow-up work to do. The day of the lighting this year, 23
November (same day as the annual Christmas crafts fair),
committee members were out in the snow because they had
found some of the lights not working. "Next year we start in
May," Shari vowed.

Individuals are invited to give committee members
some relief through the "adopt-a-cone" program, whereby
a person or business can take responsibility for decorating
one of the distinctive cone-shaped pyramids in the Petrified
Wood Garden.

These cones are what give the lighted garden its
distinctive appearance. Eclectically lit by a variety of sizes
and colors of bulbs, they look like dozens of perfectly
symmetrical Christmas trees scattered across a city block
of park.

As the appointed hour for the lighting approached, not
many people were arriving. The temperature had dipped
below zero. Those present were huddling around the heater
in the Chamber office (which used to be Ole Quammen's

gas station), sipping cider.

Then pickups and utility vehicles began pulling up, angle parking, and cutting their lights. Parents with kids got out to run around; old folks stayed in their vehicles, and Tori took

cider and cookies around to them. Considering the weather, and the circumstance that the Lemmon Cowgirls were playing for the State A consolation trophy that afternoon, the crowd was getting respectable by the time someone inside threw the switch and the fossil park came alive with light.

It wasn't a night to linger long, but once lit, the park became a drive-by attraction, as vehicles cruised deliberately by and around the block. How about a bonfire next year?

Petrified wood cone and cannonball boulder, Lemmon, South Dakota.

It's warm, at least, in the bar and grill at the north end of town, which is about a block from the North Dakota border. Much of the town has repaired here to warm up and refresh, but I find a place at the bar beside a pleasant woman. Turns out she's the wife of the barman, and hers are among the

many kids racing around the place harassing the more
serious drinkers.

Now and then she calls them down, but with little
effect, and finally she has to call in an air strike. The
publican leans over the bar and shouts, "If you kids don't
sit down and be quiet, you're gonna have to sit in the
liquor store!"

I like Lemmon.

It gets a mention in the WPA guide to North Dakota,
and that's how come I came looking for it–the St. Mary's
shrine, in New England, North Dakota. It's long gone, I
learned, but the stories are still there.

I'm looking at a postcard-photo of the shrine now. What
a fantastic place! A little mountain of petrified wood with
Our Lady of Fatima set into a recession at the top. Alongside
another structure of petrified wood, with a grotto inside, and
inside the grotto an altar ornamented with colorful quartz.
Turrets of petrified wood and round stones all over the
place, and on the highest, a cross. It's a lot like the Petrified
Wood Park in Lemmon, South Dakota. Now, how about
those stories?

All right, here's one. According to published local
histories, the first parish priest in New England was Father
Herman Regensberger. The good father gave heroic service
ministering to victims of the influenza epidemic in 1918. He
was out visiting the sick one day and, while cranking his car,
opened a cut on his knuckles. Blood poisoning set in.
Doctors wanted to amputate his hand, but Father
Regensberger said that without the hand he could not give
the mass, and then what would be the use of his life? So he
died. Now there's a story for you.

Back to the shrine, though–I knocked on the door of the local convent house of the School Sisters of Notre Dame. Sister Eleanor Zeren gave me a little of the story and sent me on to see her brother, Leo. When I went to see Leo at his home, he called up neighbor Ruth Fitterer, who brought over photos. Hospitable folks in Regent! (Plus, you get a wonderful hot beef sandwich at the Arrowhead Lanes.)

It seems the shrine stood where the St. Mary's School gymnasium now stands. "My dad gave the first $100 to help start St. Mary's School," says Leo. This was in the early 1920s, when the frame church also was enlarged. The School Sisters of Saint Mary arrived to run the school, and with them came Sister Catherine Baker–that godly woman dubbed "Catherine the Great" by local citizen Elmer Freeman, who composed a little essay about her.

He writes, "I remember being awe-struck, terrorized, amazed, proud, scared, admiring, affectionate and puzzled, all in the same hour around Sister Catherine." She believed the human spirit needed beauty, and so she started an orchestra. "Sister Catherine had a way of swishing her black habit and veil as she entered our orchestra rehearsal room that left no doubt about who was in charge," Freeman recalls. "The one luxury which she permitted herself was to break a baton about every other week when the violins messed up."

She was determined to beautify the church and school grounds, too, and so she set farmers hauling petrified wood to the school yard and recruited the artisan Joe Schwartzbauer to build what came to be called the St. Mary's School Grotto. They also ornamented the interior of the church with quartz altars and built three outdoor altars spaced about the church and school grounds, including the one in the grotto. On Rogation Sunday the congregation was led in prayer at each altar in sequence, finishing up at the grotto.

The church and school complex grew through the years, with a high school in 1948, a new brick church in 1956, and a new brick grade school in the 1970s—along with a gymnasium. The shrine was bulldozed into a hole to make way for the gym. This by no means was greeted by universal approbation among parishioners.

A few years ago the high school closed. Then I heard that the grade school was closing. I suppose the gym will still get some use. But will parents line up their kids in the gym for First Communion pictures, the way they did at the shrine?

8. A Sore Subject

My friend and colleague Dave Danbom has written about the heroic efforts of the North Dakota Agricultural Experiment Station to establish a dairy industry in North Dakota. The story he told was both sad and comic (comic mainly because of Danbom). Big-time dairying failed in North Dakota, as in most other parts of the plains, because of "intractable realities"–distance, semiaridity, lack of urban markets.

For fifty years, a symbol of the dairy crusade in North Dakota was the grave of Noble's Golden Marguerite, star milker of the station. Marguerite rested beneath a stone and plaque in front of the Dairy Building. Finally the college gave up, abolished the Dairy Department, removed the marker, and left Marguerite where she lay.

There stands still another monument to the dairy boomlet of the northern plains– Salem Sue, the World's Largest

Salem Sue, the World's Largest Cow, commemorates the New Salem Dairy Circuit–and draws traffic off Interstate 94.

Holstein. Fifty feet long, 38 feet tall, fiberglass, she stands on
School Hill, near the town of New Salem, North Dakota.
She overlooks Interstate 94, from which highway I first
spied her during a drive to Dickinson. Larry Remele, of
Bismarck, later took me out for a closer look, and his com-
rades at the State Historical Society of North Dakota
provided me with some newspaper clippings.

The Salem Sue story goes back to 1906, when pioneer
dairyman Dave Young got disgusted with the poor grade of
cows in the New Salem vicinity and decided to do something about it. He took orders from his neighbors, went over
to Wisconsin, and brought back two cars full of registered
Holsteins.

The farmers of New Salem, organized as the New Salem
Holstein Circuit, became the darlings of the dairy scientists
over at Fargo. The New Salem folks soon won renown for
fine registered Holsteins, showed them frequently, and sold
breeding stock to every other county in the state.

The schools of New Salem adopted the Holstein as their
symbol and designated black-and-white their school colors.

It was in about 1970 that someone at the bank had the
idea for a Holstein monument. The bank made the first
donation toward the project, which was organized by the
local Lions Club. The Lions raised $40,000. That paid a
firm in LaCrosse, Wisconsin (which was appropriate,
considering the source of the first Holsteins brought to
New Salem), to cast the cow from a model by an artist
named Dave Oswald. The Lions said they wanted to honor
dairymen, promote tourism, and simply have the biggest
cow in the world.

In 1974 they got Sue's hooves anchored in place on her footings. She does indeed stand majestically on the hill. But she looked pretty funny getting there.

The fiberglass sculpting company shipped her out in three sections on flatbeds. One truck hauled the head section, another the rear end. The strangest sight on the road, however, was the flatbed bearing the bottom section— four hooves and udder pointed skyward.

Over east a few miles the Jamestown, North Dakota, Chamber of Commerce, having a few thousand dollars left over from its Diamond Jubilee, decided in 1957 to erect a monument—but a monument to what? Someone suggested a shock of wheat, which was appropriate for the great spring wheat state, but no: Could you picture kids pestering their parents to pull into Jamestown so they could look at the wheat? So the Jamestown people decided on a buffalo. The city council agreed to assist with financing.

Elmer Peterson, an art professor from Jamestown College, took charge of the project, with technical assistance from an architectural firm in town. He put up a frame of 8-inch H-beams, and over that he arranged mesh wire in the form of a buffalo. Then he ran stiff concrete through a pressure hose into the mesh to make a solid, 60-ton, 26-foot-high, 46-foot-long buffalo.

The World's Largest Buffalo, they say – "to remind us of the vast herds of buffalo that roamed the prairies of North Dakota"–and to pull in traffic off Interstate 94. The buffalo, incidentally, pre-dates the touristy Frontier Village which adjoins it today.

The dedication of the Jamestown buffalo, on 4 June 1960, was unexpectedly controversial (according to clip-

pings from the State Historical Society of North Dakota). It
happened that Governor John Davis, a Republican, was
running for the United States Senate, and he brought
Governor Nelson Rockefeller out from New York to cam-
paign for him. This was a great opportunity for the
Jamestown folks. They got Rockefeller, flanked by Davis, to
speak at the dedication and thereby had the event covered
by a bemused eastern press corps.

Democrats in town were bitter. This was supposed to be
a nonpartisan, civic event, they said. Fifteen hundred
people showed up, and what they heard was a purely
political spiel. Instead of intoning platitudes about pioneers and the passing of the prairie, Rockefeller lit into the
Democrats and so praised Governor Davis as to make him
loom, politically, large as the buffalo. One of the Democrats
(who were, admittedly, few) said that perhaps the town
should have put up an elephant, not a buffalo.

It almost seemed as though Governor Rockefeller was
running for something himself. He arrived a little late, like
someone with the busy agenda of a statesman, and then
pitched into the crowd, shaking hands, donning an Indian
headdress, shaking hands, eating a buffalo burger, shaking
hands. Lots of photo opportunities, as the press people say.

In Jamestown, Governor Rockefeller was also supposed
to deliver a "major agriculture speech," but a local reporter
said afterward that it "wasn't very major." There even was
some question as to whether the buffalo burger he ate was
bona fide. (The Chamber cooks admitted that most of the
burgers were beef.)

The governor did score a few points by remarking that
his sons were married to good Norwegian girls. Which had

about as much to do with the buffalo as everything else that
went on.

It is to me an irony that the walleye has become a
favorite fish, almost a sacred fish, to the sporting public on
the Great Plains. I remember what an oddity it seemed the
first time I accidentally caught one at a reservoir in western
Kansas.

The walleye would be of no account on the plains were
it not for the U.S. Army Corps of Engineers and its Pick-
Sloan plan. So, you happy trollers, be careful how you cuss
the federal government.

The Mecca for walleye-worshipers on the plains is the
upper Missouri, with its great triumvirate, lakes Oahe,
Sakakawea, and Fort Peck, backing up across the Dakotas
and Montana. The town of Garrison, North Dakota, on
the shore of Sakakawea, has marked this distinction with a
monument–Wally the Walleye.

He was supposed to be Willy the Walleye. I got this
story from Les Korgel, the McLean County treasurer. It was
the late W.C. "Bud" Parker, owner of a tavern and other
businesses in Garrison, who had the great idea of erecting a
walleye monument. The Garrison Civic Club, the North
Dakota Governor's Walleye Cup, the Garrison Sportsman's
Club, and the Garrison Jaycees all got behind the project,
raising $14,000.

They contracted with the Pietsch Sign Company of
Minot to cast a 26-foot fiberglass fish and mount him in
the Kenneth S. Fitzsimmons Memorial Mini-Park at the
north end of Main. Over at the city office I found Diane
Affeldt, the City Auditor, who fished the original sketch
out of a file for me to examine.

Willy was to be the monster's name, until the local
promoters discovered that a Minnesota town—by coinci-
dence, a town also named Garrison—already had a giant
walleye named Willy. Hence Wally.

Wally was installed in May 1980. Since then, Les says,
"A lot of pictures have been taken of people with fishing
rods, hooked to the largest walleye in the world." Billboards
bearing Wally's likeness proclaim Garrison the "Walleye
Capital of the World." This may not affect the standing of
Garrison as a destination point for fishermen, but business
people say it pulls quite a few travelers off the highway and
into their businesses.

Twice Wally has been taken down for refurbishment.
On his second return, in 1994, the town held a "Welcome
Home" parade. You can buy a Wally the Walleye Restora-
tion Fund pin for $3.00.

He's brightly colored in green and yellow, and he is
indeed wall-eyed—big blank white eyes, like a freshman
history student late in the semester.

Wait a minute, I'm studying the big fish, and what's
that rising above it to the north? The two Garrison city
water towers, one marked "Hot" and the other "Cold."
Puckish folk, these Garrisonians.

Diane says the city had a contractor sand-blasting the
towers, and he asked the town fathers if they wanted any
legend painted on them. It was he who suggested "Hot" and
"Cold." I wonder if this same contractor did the job in
Canton, Kansas?

The first person in Harvey, North Dakota, I asked
about the gorilla out on 52 Highway said, "It's a sore

subject with a lot of people." Sounds like a story, I thought. So here it is.

Once there was this gorilla named Og, or rather a chest-up bust of a gorilla–30 feet tall, arms upraised in menace (45 feet elbow to elbow), pearly teeth (serious overbite), red eyes that moved. He was built in 1978 by a fellow named Bob Watts, in Dickinson–steel frame, chicken-wire shell, plastic skin, wool (if that's what you call gorilla-hair) of insulation material.

Og lived first in a frontier-fort tourist trap, Rawhide City, in Mandan. He stood there to commemorate the many gorillas who helped to win the west.

After Rawhide City went belly up in 1984, Og was purchased by Glen Lelm, of Harvey. He planned to put the gorilla, emblazoned with a company logo, atop Lelm Implement, but his insurance company didn't like the idea. So for years Og was scrapped out back.

Along came Bert Miller, 62 years a clothier in Harvey, public-spirited as they come. He was tired of having to explain where Harvey was–the nondescript little town just off the highway between Jamestown and Minot. No, not the place with the big Indian, that's Carrington, and no, not the place with the pretty fairgrounds, that's Fessenden.

In 1993 Bert, without much help, retrieved Og from Lelm's and set him up on a platform along the highway. Og got some patching and a new paint job. Bert put up some highway signs that said, "Come into Harvey and Monkey around." He also planted some lilacs around the platform, which ought to appeal to those sensitive folk who think Og is too brutish for their community.

"I pretty near got run out of Harvey for a while," Bert says. A homemaker's club changed his signs to say, "Not even a

Og the Gorilla T-shirts put Harvey, North Dakota, on the map.

gorilla can defeat a Harvey Hornet" (the high-school mascot). Everybody had an opinion. But you know, it's no longer difficult to remind people where Harvey is.

It probably would be possible to design a more aesthetically pleasing gorilla than Og, but in this post-modern era, I'm not going to try to arbitrate public taste. (Besides, I'm biased, because Bert sent me an Og T-shirt.) Nor am I too concerned with those citizens who think that a gorilla is too undignified for their fair city. It doesn't hurt them to be stirred up a little.

No, what intrigues me is the idea of a GORILLA on the open plains, peeking through the lilacs. Maybe even a gorilla in the mist, as Jim Lelm, gazing across from the implement company, says Og appears particularly impressive when there is a haze stealing in from the slough.

The plains are heavily populated with roadside monstrosities, but nearly all of them are what you could call indigenous creatures—a concrete prairie dog in Oakley, Kansas, a dinosaur in Drumheller, Alberta, a cowboy in Canyon, Texas, a buffalo in Jamestown, North Dakota, and so on.

Can we accept an African gorilla in our midst (or mist)? Why not? We've already got Russian wheats, Japanese pickups, Norwegian Lutherans, and espresso bars.

9. They Wanted a Viking

Maybe it's because Euro-American settlement is so recent that modern residents of the Great Plains are so passionate about their antiquities. People want to have predecessors. They find a piece of rusty iron in a plowed field, and they conclude right off that it is chain mail lost by Coronado. If you look at them long enough, ATV tracks across pastures start to look like Santa Fe or Oregon trail ruts.

When you get into those localities settled by Scandinavians–Swedes, Norwegians, Danes, Icelanders–Norsemen are the predecessors of choice. Many a summer-cabin resident in Minnesota believes in his heart that where he now trolls for walleye, Viking vessels once plied in exploration.

Quite a bit of this Viking-consciousness spills into the Dakotas. Out in Fort Ransom, North Dakota, in the beautiful Sheyenne River valley, Snorri Thorfinnson spoke for those who insisted that Norsemen had been there centuries before.

Thorfinnson, who was of Icelandic descent, served as county agricultural agent for nearby Sargent County before retiring to Fort Ransom, in Ransom County. There he wrote a county history and a book of poems and investigated local antiquities.

Thorfinnson believed that certain hills in the Sheyenne valley were Hopewellian Indian mounds. He also contended that certain boulders on the valley slopes were, in fact, mooring stones for Viking ships, and that others bore Norse inscriptions. He suggested that visiting Norsemen taught the Mandan Indians to build houses of timber. They also left among the Mandan the genetic traits of blue eyes and red hair. (Others have argued these came from wandering Celts, and the Vikings were relative late-comers.)

So, in about 1970, several folks in Fort Ransom, a Norwegian settlement, inspired by the example of the world's largest buffalo in Jamestown, decided that Fort Ransom should have a monument to the Norse explorers. One of them, Lowell Johnson, made a wood-carving as a model. Thorfinnson and an artist friend, Bjarne Ness, started taking lessons in sculpture. But Ness got cancer, and they didn't think they could complete the project.

Ultimately the Fort Ransom Commercial Club got a young Vietnam veteran named Bill Woell to take it on. He

built a metal frame and plastered it with a sort of burlap-mache. His monumental Viking was slender, about fourteen feet tall, replete with sword, spear, breastplate, and horned helmet. He had a full beard and handlebar mustache and the most diabolical eyes. The club got a helicopter to place the statue atop one of the Indian mounds overlooking town.

The Black Viking of Fort Ransom, North Dakota.

I've talked with Thorfinnson's local descendants and with Bjarne Ness's widow, Anne, about this. I know that reaction to the Viking monument was distinctly mixed. The spear looked like a pitchfork, and the horned helmet, combined with the wild eyes, made the thing all too devil-ish. "They wanted a Viking," says Mrs. Ness, "but not that kind."

The guy wires on the Viking are loose, his sword is broken, he's in general disrepair, and no one seems to care. One Halloween some boys hauled an old privy up the hillside and set it next to the monument. Mostly, the townsfolk just ignore it. It doesn't look the way they want their Norse forbears to look.

As a community monument, it doesn't work. As a piece of primitive, eccentric folk-art, it's outstanding. I suspect that one of these days a hard north wind is going to topple it.

You probably haven't noticed (or cared), but in the opening sequence of the movie *Wayne's World*, as the camera pans a street scene, you get a glimpse of a giant Indian, maybe 25 feet tall, set up on top of some business. The reason I noticed (and care) is that I know where that Indian's brother is. He's standing in front of the Chieftain Motel, in Carrington, North Dakota. Jud and Gen Tracy put him there in 1965.

I'm going somewhere with this, and it has to do with the story of most every town on the plains. Most of our towns were founded as railroad towns, but over time, those that have survived have become highway towns.

That's how hotels became obsolete. Every town had a hotel or two near the railway station. Most of them are gone now, and where they remain, they are no longer used as hotels. In my old hometown of Ellinwood, Kansas, for instance, the Wolf Hotel, across from the Santa Fe depot, is an antique store.

In the early 1920s Jud's father, Don Tracy, ran such a hotel—the Linton Hotel, in Linton, North Dakota. Among his guests was the young Lawrence Welk, who shared a room and bed with his drummer; Jud showed me the register. When the hotel burned down, Don Tracy bought a movie theater in Carrington. After the second world war his son came home to Carrington with his bride, and they bought the Garland Hotel.

This was already late to buy a hotel. The lodging business largely had moved onto the highway, into the Rainbow Gardens. This was a stucco cabin court, beautifully and whimsically landscaped by a Japanese-American proprietor, who unfortunately was interned during the war.

Jud and Gen sold the hotel in 1948, ran a restaurant downtown for eight years, and then bought a ten-stool diner on the highway. They expanded it and named it the "Big Chief Cafe." When they bought the A & W, they named it the "Little Chief Drive-In." They had caught on that an American Indian motif was a good hook for the cross-country tourist trade.

Thus in 1964, when they built their new motel-restaurant, it was christened "The Chieftain." The restaurant featured the Big Chief Belly Buster, a giant hamburger. Times were good for highway service businesses: "We had U.S. 52 (which is transcontinental) and U.S. 281 (which is transcontinental), plus N.D. 200 running east and west from Minnesota into Montana," explains Jud. "There was a lot of traffic."

But what about the big fiberglass Indian out front? Jud saw one like it in front of the Thunderbird Motel, on the south side of Minneapolis, and said to the owner, "Rodney, where did you get that big Indian out front? I have to have one of those!"

The manufacturer, in California, was happy to oblige. The company sold its monstrous figures in modular form. The legs of all were the same, but the top could be either an Indian or a cowboy, whichever you ordered. Obviously, the company sold at least three of the Indian model–the one in Minneapolis, the one in Carrington, and the one in *Wayne's World*.

Jud and Gen–Gen ran the restaurant–had the Chieftain for ten years before selling and retiring. It's still a flourishing enterprise.

I came away from my visit carrying a memento–the recipe for Gen's famous Chieftain beer cheese soup, made from butter, chicken stock, grated carrots and celery and onions, parsley, cheddar cheese, and a couple pints of Budweiser. The proportions are large, but next time I need to serve 200 guests, I'll be ready.

Wish luck to the boys down in Regent, North Dakota, because they've erected the third set of sculptures on the Enchanted Highway. And they're big–a Pheasant Family: a rooster, a hen, and three chicks, the rooster measuring 30 feet tall and 60 feet long. The technical part, construction and assembly, the guys can handle. Luck or something like it comes in when you consider the high aspirations they hold for their humble creations.

By now they have some experience in this sort of thing. In 1994 they built the Tin Family, and in 1995 they

set it up alongside the blacktop road running from
Gladstone to Regent, which they now style the Enchanted
Highway. The same year, they erected that marvelous
silhouette, "Teddy Rides Again"–the old roughrider himself
on a rearing horse.

This is one of those wonderful wild hairs that spring up
here and there on the plains. I got the story first from
Brenda Wiseman, who runs the Co-op Store in Regent and
is on the Enchanted Highway board of directors. Then I
called up Gary Greff, who everyone says is the guiding
spirit in the effort.

Gary was a schoolteacher and a principal in Poplar,
Montana, when he called it quits in 1991 and came home
to Regent. "I guess I was always sort of an entrepreneur,"
he says. While incubating other enterprises, he got going
on the Enchanted Highway.

The idea originated when Alan Honeyman of Stoney
Butte Ranch made a haybale man and set it up along the
road. This attracted so much public interest that Gary got
to thinking what might be done along such lines to put the
community on the map. "What are we good at here?", he
thought. "We're good at metal, at welding."

Idle talk in the coffee shops turned to action in the
welding shops. Gary and a bunch of farmers, ranchers, and
Regent residents decided to promote the Gladstone-Regent
corridor from I-94 by spacing ten sculpture sites along its
thirty-mile length. They came up with ideas, which Gary's
architect brother helped to draw up.

I went to the site of the Tin Family and looked it over,
while a pair of curlew buzzed my head and screamed
angrily at Bancroft the History Dog. The figures are massive conglomerations of salvage, the largest, the Tin Man

and Tin Lady, 44 feet tall. The Tin Lady has barb-wire hair and augur-screw earrings. The Tin Boy looks a heck of a lot like Bart Simpson. Their feet are cattle tanks.

Whereas the Tin Family is whimsical, Teddy Rides Again is monumental. Fifty-one feet tall, this black-pipe silhouette is striking against the blue sky. The wind makes pop-bottle music as it blows over the pipe ends.

Tin Boy, on the Enchanted Highway, near Regent, North Dakota.

The Pheasant Family is constructed of gravel screen attached to well pipe frames. It's notable that each sculpture site on the Enchanted Highway uses a completely different set of designs and techniques. Coming up next: the World's Largest Grasshopper.

Now, the Great Plains are strewn with roadside art, but what sets the Enchanted Highway apart is the audacity and collaboration involved. Sixty or more people have been involved in building sculptures, getting together in a shop in Regent. The labor and many of the materials are donated, but it still costs about $10,000 to set up a site—money for cement, primer, and other materials not available by donation. The state arts council, the local Lions, and other donors help out with a continuous community fund drive.

The official documents of the Enchanted Highway committee say its purposes are to promote tourism and to "provide an outlet for artistic expression for the people involved." Gary says, "We're trying to figure out some way to keep Regent alive." He envisions sculpture gardens in town and metal-art store fronts. He wants to see Regent hailed as the Metal Art Capital of the World. He has, he confesses, "more dreams than Carter has pills."

Sceptics, go take a look for yourselves.

10. Big Birds

Bringing ringneck pheasants to the American plains was a great idea. The native grouse–sharptails and prairie chickens–passed with the breaking of the prairie and survive only where large expanses of native grassland remain. Ringnecks, on the other hand, thrive in grain farming country. So do Hungarian partridge, but they haven't spread and prospered over so much of the plains as have the pheasants.

Pheasants are a great thing for the hospitality industry. Check the South Dakota lodging section of a AAA guide, and you'll find that motels in pheasant country double their rates for the hunting season.

A bird this important deserves commemoration. From Kansas to North Dakota you find establishments with names like "Ringneck Bar & Grill" and "Pheasant Lounge," marked by likenesses of the gamebird rendered in bright paints and neon.

I thought I had found all the more official monuments to the ringneck. I knew about the world's largest pheasant, atop the liquor store in the Plains Motel parking lot of Huron, South Dakota, and I knew about the pheasant-on-a-stick in downtown Redfield, South Dakota. Then Joanita Kant Monteith told me about Tinkertown.

Tinkertown is a piece of roadside Americana. It arose on the northwest corner of highways 22 and 212, just west of Watertown, South Dakota. It was the creation of Emma and Willis Walters.

In 1948 the Walters moved a building called the Old
Dane Hall to the corner and began using it for a gas station
and lunch counter.

Willis, in particular,
had grand ideas
about the future of
the business, and he
was aware of the
importance of
pheasant season to
his trade.

Tinkertown, along Highway 212 west of
Watertown, South Dakota.

So he welded
some pipe into a
frame and around it sculpted, from concrete, a giant pheasant, about 8 feet tall and 15 feet long. The bird is a bit
stylistic; the tail is too straight and too thick, but these
defects are owing to the nature of the materials. A ladder
leaned against the bird's side, and a saddle placed on his
neck, offered kids a ride and parents a photo opportunity.

There were other attractions. Willis also sculpted the
life-size "Depression Nag" and hitched to it the old mail
wagon from Garden City, South Dakota. In 1958 they
moved in the Kampeska Methodist Church and made it
into a museum. This wasn't very successful, and so they
converted it into an antique and souvenir store. They also
had a little menagerie in cages—skunks, rabbits, foxes.

The Walters ran the place until 1980, when Willis
died. Emma still lives in Watertown, but she doesn't much
want to talk about Tinkertown. "It was a tourist trap, that
was all," she says. The concrete pheasant and horse still
stand in good shape. A welder has opened a shop in the
buildings.

Pheasant hunters and other travelers remember the place well. Joanita (who is Executive Director of the Codington County Historical Society) recalls stopping there on her father's hunting expeditions. She has a photograph labeled, "Tinkertown opening hunting day, 1949," and showing, along with the big bird, her mother, sister, and brother.

I don't know why I'm such a sucker for places like this. I should find something more seriously historical to occupy my time.

Jim and I were in Sioux Falls on a weekend in October that happened to be the opening weekend of pheasant season. Into the hotel lobby came all sorts of guys from the Twin Cities and Des Moines and who knows where decked out in mail-order hunting gear that is supposed to be impervious to any organic substance. The day was warm, and I knew pretty soon those chubby birddogs waiting in the parking lot would be worn out.

Still, as we drove off toward home, I sort of wished I could hang around. Lines of fellows were stomping across the stubble fields. Local kids were walking the bar ditches. In a cafe where we stopped, someone had hung an advertisement offering to clean pheasants for so-much-a-bird. A ritual was taking place. Thousands of urban Nimrods were making their annual escape to the freedom of the flatlands.

South Dakota long has billed itself as the "Pheasant Capital of the World." In his superb bulletin, *History, Ecology and Management of the Ring-Necked Pheasant in South Dakota*, Carl G. Trautman recalls the "good old pheasant years" from the 1930s to the early 1960s. "In addition to the robust conviviality, anticipation and excitement of the hunt," he writes, "there were spectacles of pheasants galore, fabulous nimrod success, more-than-usual ringing of cash registers, aroma of pheasant in the frying pan, varied and colorful autumn scenes, and communion with nature."

South Dakota was the place to go. I have copies of some wonderful home movies of doctors and dentists and their dogs from Emporia, Kansas, shooting and shooting in the Pheasant Capital state during the 1940s. I'm keeping them for their historic value.

The ringneck pheasant flourished on the central and northern plains because it had good habitat and was itself adaptable. The pheasant came to North America with mixed ancestry—it was not a pure Chinese ringneck, but one crossed with European fowl and probably other Asian pheasants. Its genetic diversity helped it fit into various conditions on the plains.

Those conditions were favorable for a long time. Farming was not too intensive. First the hardships of the 1930s caused abandonment of many fields from cultivation. Next the shortages of World War II prevented fencerow-to-fencerow farming. And then the Soil Bank program put land back into grass. Pheasants and pheasant hunting prospered.

The pheasant boom in South Dakota collapsed in 1964. During the early 1940s the estimated number of pheasants in the state was in the 16 to 30 million range, whereas in later years it was closer to 2 million. Some say that the end of the Soil Bank and the advent of more intensive farming caused this. Others insist that the ringneck has degenerated as a species, losing its genetic diversity and hardiness. (The former explanation seems more likely to me. I can't see blaming things on the birds.) The annual hunt continues, however, and makes its mark on the culture of the plains.

Other places on the plains sometimes challenge the designation of South Dakota as the Pheasant Capital. No claims (to my knowledge) come from states south of Kansas, because the habitat for ringnecks gets more and more marginal as you go south from the sunflower state.

Norton, in northwestern Kansas, calls itself the Pheasant Capital of the World, but either the folks at Norton are just big talkers or they think the Kansas border is the edge of the world. States to the north have far more pheasants.

Nebraska, for instance. That state had its first pheasant season in 1927. My *Nebraskaland* history of outdoor life in Nebraska calls the 1930s "The Heyday of the Ringneck." Field abandonment during that decade produced a profusion of pheasants in Nebraska, just as in South Dakota. In 1936, however, the state prohibited hunting in certain areas. Farmers insisted that they needed the pheasants in the fields to combat the grasshopper plague of that year.

No town in Nebraska (again, to my knowledge) claims to be the city for pheasants, but two towns in South Dakota do—Redfield and Huron. Redfield has a logical argument for its self-designation as the Pheasant Capital of the World: the Chamber of Commerce says the Redfield vicinity was "Where the popular Chinese Ringneck Pheasants were first successfully stocked."

This isn't just public-relations hype, for literature from the South Dakota State Game, Fish, and Parks Department substantially confirms the Redfield claim. The local pheasant population began with private releases by several Redfield men in 1908; the Chamber of Commerce and the state followed up with larger releases in 1911, and the first local pheasant population took hold.

The Chamber of Commerce has a fetching ringneck on its letterhead, but the more visible symbol of Redfield's affinity for the pheasant is the big bird: a fiberglass ring-neck, well-proportioned, realistically painted, perhaps twenty feet long, beak to tail. Surrounded by landscaping and benches, alongside United States and South Dakota flags, the big bird sits atop a pole near the intersection of two highways in Redfield. He never roosts; floodlights illuminate him by night.

Redfield, as its contribution to the state centennial in 1989, erected a marker alongside the fiberglass pheasant detailing how the imported gamebird was established in the area.

The World's Largest Pheasant has perched atop the Plains Liquor Store of Huron, South Dakota, since 1959.

The Redfield ring-neck is not the largest pheasant facsimile in the world, however, or even the largest in South Dakota. That honor belongs to the fiberglass pheasant in Huron.

Now, the Huron bird is not an aesthetic delight. Its posture is wrong, with its broad chest stuck out and its head drawn back. If you're familiar with

pheasants, and you're familiar with turkeys, you'd say the
Huron bird holds himself more like the latter than the
former.

Still, the World's Largest Pheasant, which stands on a
pedestal in the Plains Motel parking lot in Huron, is a big
bird. Twenty-eight feet high, about forty from beak to tail.
The sculptor (in fiberglass on a steel frame) was one Robert
Jacobs, of Goodring, Idaho.

Here is the story (gleaned from clippings sent me by
the Huron Public Library) behind the bird. The Junior
Chamber of Commerce sponsored his creation as a promo-
tion for the town of Huron. The Jaycees dedicated him on
October 16, 1959, with 2,500 spectators present, if you
count the ones who sat in their cars.

Dignitaries attended. The main speaker was former
governor Joe Foss, an ardent hunter, but Senator Francis
Case and Representative George McGovern made a few
remarks, too. Also on the program were the director of the
state game, fish, and parks department; the mayor of Huron;
some people from the Chamber of Commerce; and Bill
Bauer, Jr., of Wisconsin, who had been chosen as a representative hunter from out-of-state.

Senator Case told the Jaycees that their bird was destined to become a symbol of the state of South Dakota on a
par with Mount Rushmore.

Former governor Foss, the keynoter, departed after the
ceremony by helicopter, and as he did, he pointed his
shotgun out and fired a few blanks at the fiberglass pheasant.

In retrospect, however, the comments made at the
ceremony by Representative McGovern are most interesting. This took place right after the big-time farmer from

Iowa, Roswell Garst, had brought Premier Nikita Khrushchev of the Soviet Union over to visit the United States. Khrushchev had been bragging all through the trip about how the corn in Russia was better than the corn in Iowa and so on.

So, in Huron, McGovern was quoted as saying, "I wish he [Khrushchev] could see this bird. I'm sure there isn't one like it in Russia."

The significance of this evidently off-hand statement may not be obvious, but remember that the ringneck pheasant is a Chinese bird. What better way to send a message to the Soviet premier than to direct his attention upon a monument to a Chinese bird erected in the heartland of the U.S.A.?

When McGovern ran for President in 1972, people said he didn't know anything about foreign affairs. Not so, for here in 1959, long before Richard Nixon even thought about it, McGovern was playing the China card, right in the middle of the Plains Motel parking lot.

I wrote Mr. McGovern, now retired from the United States Senate, about the incident. Ping-pong diplomacy was nothing compared to this, I said. I asked him how he arrived at this advanced position of diplomacy in 1959 and what effects it had on his career and on the general course of American foreign policy.

Mr. McGovern never answered. Another thing they said back in 1972 was that he didn't have any sense of humor.

11. Thresherman's Heaven

Old 81 Highway is a border road. Crossing Oklahoma and Kansas north and south, it is commonly regarded as the symbolic line that divides eastern Oklahoma from western Oklahoma, eastern Kansas from western Kansas. Follow it across Nebraska, and it keeps you skirting the east edge of the sandhills. Across the Dakotas, 81 demarcates the urban eastern fringe from the rural balance of state. If I travel 81 too long, I feel ill at ease, because like Woodrow Call in *Lonesome Dove*, I "despise the border and long for the open plains."

Nevertheless, I kind of like Watertown, South Dakota. Get some gas at the Cowboy Convenience Store (big fiberglass cowboy out front, remember I'm a sucker for that stuff), have a burger at the Office bar and grill, where the waitresses have tenure.

It's the approach from the south that gets me in a good mood about Watertown, though. Prominent atop a hill on the lefthand side of the highway is Corson Emminger's round barn.

Corson Emminger came out from Wisconsin and bought his farm south of Watertown in 1905. In 1909-10, at a cost of some $1500, he built the remarkable barn that still slows traffic on old 81. The barn is about fifty feet in diameter, with high walls and a steep roof. It was constructed of concrete blocks, which were left unpainted for most of its life. Now they are painted white, which sets off the green asphalt-shingle roof in striking fashion.

In earlier days the barn would have been even more impressive than it is today, because earthen ramps ascended to the two big loft doors, one on the north and one on the south. The ramps allowed teams and wagons to deliver hay and grain into the loft.

Emminger owned the place for only four years after building the barn. He sold it to Jacob Krull, who had it for almost thirty years. There have been several owners since, including the current ones, the Moeller family.

The Moellers bought the place in 1972 and remodeled the barn as a dairy facility, installing milking stalls on the ground level. Lowell Moeller, who worked in the barn, said its design had advantages on the northern plains. "It isn't a cold barn," he told a reporter. "The snow is left in a circle about twenty or thirty feet from the barn. We never have to worry about having a door snowed shut."

Currently the barn is not used for anything except storage. It is the only round barn in South Dakota on the National Register of Historic Places. (The Historic Preservation Department of the state historical society helped me out with information.)

I entered the barn via the milkhouse, passed through the milking-stall area, and climbed a ladder into the loft. English sparrows flitted about the inside of the cupola above, where a bit of light came in. The doors were tied shut; I worked one loose to admit more light (and so that later I could jump down to the ground).

The loft is tall and ample; it would hold a lot of hay. I couldn't figure out the pulley system for hay handling; something must be missing. In the four corners–whoops, I guess there aren't any corners–at four points 90 degrees from one another are square-cornered granaries.

You can climb on top of the granaries, where planks running from one to another make a second loft level. You could have fun in this barn, and probably break some bones. I wish I could have got both loft doors open to let the wind blow through.

Some folks call him Wild Bill, more call him Rumely Bill. He's a collector, and the creator of a head-turning roadside monument. He's Bill Krumwiede, from Voltaire, North Dakota.

It's a common custom up and down the plains to pull old separators, or threshing machines, onto hills alongside highways where they can be viewed by travelers. These are folk monuments, calling

The threshing machine on the hill—a folk monument to hard work.

on us to remember the hard work of harvests past.

Rumely Bill takes this to the extreme. He's pulled thirty separators onto two adjacent hills along Highway 52 southeast of Velva. The Valley of the Dinosaurs, some people call the place; others call it Thresherman's Heaven.

"My dad had the first threshing rig around here," says Bill, who commenced service as straw monkey of the outfit. "My dad and brother Edward and I threshed for over forty years for the same neighbors."

During World War II Bill was a 1st Class Gunner's Mate on a destroyer. When he came home, his father gave him a

1916 Rumely oil-pull tractor—which maybe was a mistake, as it started Bill down the road of collecting things. He resolved to collect all sixteen models of Rumely oil-pulls, and by 1981 he had them all.

Over the years, he's also collected traps (a collection of untold thousands), western novels (5000 of them in the basement), guns (a collection now dispersed), Model A Fords (bought ten of them one year), and nobody knows quite how many acres of land.

And then there are those separators down on the highway. "I was going to put them out here in the yard, but I thought, what's the use?" Bill explains. "It would do some good for people to see them up there and smile."

And remember the satisfactions of exhaustion. "Threshing was terrible hard work. You could thresh until you were played out. Then you could sit down and have a sandwich, and when you got up, you were young again."

Now Bill's son, Bill Jr., from Hazen, helps him wrestle his threshing monuments up the hill. He still has a few more to take out, and there may be no end to it. "People all know Wild Bill Krumwiede collects them and likes to see them up there. All I know is, I'm glad they're up there instead of in the yard." (Across the table, Ellen Krumwiede catches my eye and nods agreement for her own reasons.)

Shadd Piehl, a fine poet, grew up in Velva and wrote the poem, "Harvest Time," about Thresherman's Heaven. The poem captures one of the peculiar features of folk monuments such as this—their anonymity, as far as the traveling public is concerned. He writes, "Someone has brought them here as monuments." I have never seen alongside any such exhibition a sign saying who owned the threshing machine or who put it there.

Shadd says,

> These wrecks are Dakotan lamentations
> Mourning the stubble of necessary past—
> Harvesting time, threshing the years.

Bill says, "It's been a wonderful life."

Traveling the plains the past few years I've noticed an increase in roadside monuments, objects placed alongside the highway to be noticed by passing motorists. And it seems to me that the character of this stuff has changed, too. Until fairly recently most of it was commercial—a colossal cowboy advertising a gas station, a giant buffalo promoting a town—but now I see more and more folk monuments placed by individuals for their own personal reasons.

In wheat country such as Kansas, the Dakotas, or Saskatchewan, the most prominent folk monument along the highway is the old grain separator, or threshing machine, situated on a hillside. In ranch country the monument of choice, more and more, is the cowboy boot placed soles up atop a fencepost. I've seen them in western Oklahoma and Kansas, all the way up to Saskatchewan, but most of all in the Nebraska sandhills.

I subscribe to a computer listserv, or discussion group, devoted to the study of the American West and was interested when a fellow from the Smithsonian Institution asked why people out west were putting boots on fenceposts. Various writers then offered explanations like keeping rain off the posts or frightening coyotes, none of them with any basis. The truth is there isn't any practical reason for putting the boots there. You do it for personal satisfaction and to say something to the world.

Roadside monument and conversation piece near Arthur, North Dakota.

I was driving along North Dakota Highway 18 south of Arthur and noticed a line of fifty-seven boots on fenceposts. So I stopped at the house, that of Elmer and Ardy Wilhelm, and asked what was going on.

It seems they're semi-retired farmers who winter in Mesa, Arizona–keep a mobile home down there. Coming home from Arizona a few years ago, they saw boots on fenceposts in Kansas and Nebraska, and Elmer says, "I thought, I'm going to do that along the highway. And pretty soon everybody started dropping off boots." He started with six pairs of his own. Now some people just leave old boots by the mailbox to be added to the collection. Elmer and Ardy give directions to their place by saying, "Right south of town where the boots are."

"We've had a lot of fun with them," Ardy allows. "They've been a conversation piece." One day she found a couple of fellows taking boots off the posts, and she says, "Boy, did I let them have it."

The thing is, this part of North Dakota is wheat country, with not much livestock at all. Elmer has always been a farmer, but thought of himself differently–"I always called myself a rancher," he says, and always wore cowboy boots.

So what's the thought behind the boots on fenceposts, I asked? "Just retiring 'em, I guess," Elmer replies. "I don't wear 'em any more–too hard on my feet."

He's a little worried because Ardy thinks they should move to town; their son now farms the place. Elmer thinks moving to town is moving "to the dungeon." Sounds like he retires his boots easier than he retires himself.

Having pulled the tail of the world's largest pheasant, stood in the shadow of the world's largest cow, and inspected roadside monstrosities from Texas to Alberta, I thought I had seen some wonderfully ugly things. But nothing, I know now, as ugly as the Can Pile.

While Jim was up here in North Dakota one fall, we got the story. To begin, I showed him the Can Pile itself–a leaning, sagging tower near forty feet tall (they say it used to stand fifty feet), constructed of–you guessed it–quart oil cans, of the Sinclair variety. It's just south of Interstate 94 at Casselton, North Dakota. Before the interstate, this was on old Highway 10.

With a little help from friendly public librarians, we got hold of Rusty Taubert, mayor of Casselton. It turns out his uncle, Max Taubert, a bachelor and World War I veteran, built the Can Pile.

Actually, he built a gas station he called the Brick House, in 1933, and a few years later put in a lunch counter. He did a great business with truckers hauling cattle to the West Fargo stockyards.

Every time Max sold a quart or change of oil, he tossed the empty cans into a pile enclosed in a round, chicken-wire-and-web-wire enclosure. When it was full, he put

another circular layer atop the first. The layers built up,
wedding-cake-like, fifty feet high. Max put a wind generator
on top to run his pumps and, like everybody else, took to
calling his station the Can Pile. Into the bottom of the pile,
he built a sort of shed in which he kept his pigeons, homers
and tumblers.

In 1936 he added a counter, four stools, and a table and
started selling hamburgers. He hired Isolie Low and Alice
Royce to run the lunch counter during the day. Alice
worked there nineteen years. Darned if Jim and I didn't find
her, living in a nice apartment above the bank.

Max, she and others agree, was his own man. Alice
would quit, or Max would fire her, but he would apologize
and she would come back. She liked joshing the truckers
and observing the people passing through—"I just looked
forward to go to work," she says. She remembers the day a
customer emptied his ash tray on the drive. Max swept up
the contents and tossed them into the front seat of the car.

The Brick House Special was a hamburger of two
patties with a thick slice of onion fried in-between, served
with pickles and mustard. Young folks would come out for
burgers after dances. Max kept the pickles in kegs, and
nobody liked to reach in for them, because of the scum on
top.

Max's mustard was homemade and notorious. Alice gave
me the recipe, written on the back of an old Can Pile
receipt: 2 pounds dry mustard, 2 tablespoons salt, 3 tablespoons sugar, 1 teaspoon pepper, and 1 1/2 tablespoons
powdered horseradish, mixed with vinegar and no water.

Our quest for the story of the Can Pile eventually led us
to the Red Baron Lounge in downtown Casselton, where

the barmaid was real helpful. Her dad lived above the bar. She ran upstairs and came back with a postcard of the Can Pile in its heyday that she lent me so I could have a copy made.

It seems like you can turn over any rock in Casselton and find a story about the Can Pile under it. It sure is ugly, but the stories are beautiful.

12. Every One a Greenhead

Growing up in western Kansas I had a few unhappy brushes with skunks, but I never went looking for them on purpose. From what I'm told by Ernie Zahn, of Velva, North Dakota, though, skunk hunting was a pretty lucrative, if aromatic, occupation for his generation on the plains. "Skunks were the number one fur-bearer in the country," he explains. "They were worth from $2.50 to $5.00 apiece. They were graded short-stripe, long-stripe, and broad-stripe, and the shorter and darker the skunk, the more it was worth."

Ernie Zahn, retired professional hunter, with trophies of his career.

Ernie was born in 1915 to a German-Russian farm family in Dickey County, North Dakota, the twelfth of thirteen children, and his father died when he was just three. So he and his brothers did all sorts of things to make a little money and carry the family through.

"The first thing we would do in the fall,"

he says, "after the season opened November 1, was hit the culverts to take the skunks out. We would start at 12:00 midnight, and then we would go all night and all day.

"We got very efficient about this. We would go to a culvert, and in fifteen or twenty minutes we could have the skunks out and be on our way and find another one. We had equipment fixed up to get the skunks out; we had barbed wire we would wind into the skunk's hide or tail and pull it out. We got as high as sixteen skunks from a culvert, so this was big business."

How big? Ernie says, "One night we went out and we had forty-three skunks by morning, at three or four dollars apiece." Darned good wages for the 1930s.

The job was not without risk, though. Once he and a brother checked out a particular spot and, he recalls, "We looked in this culvert and it was full of skunks. But the township crew had mucked one end of the culvert shut." The skunks were way at the plugged end, wedged in tight, and the boys couldn't get them out. So they dug out the end of the culvert.

Then, "My brother, who was older than I was, he had a lot of guts, he would get down and throw the skunks out. Then he got to one and he couldn't get it. He braced his feet and he gave another pull, and when he let up, the skunk let go and scented him right in the face. He went over backwards, couldn't get his breath, he couldn't see, and he hollered, 'He got me!'

"I went down and grabbed him by the hand and led him up onto the road, opened up the pitcock on our Model T, drained some water out of the radiator, he washed his face and we sat around until he recovered. But we made forty or forty-five dollars for that bit of work."

Believe it or not, Ernie found a woman who overlooked his skunk-hunting proclivities and saw enough virtues to marry him. One fall he drove his wife over to the industrial school in Ellendale to get her teaching certificate renewed. On the way home he cruised some fields and coulees for skunks, digging into three dens and taking eighteen skunks.

When he got home, a fur buyer drove into the yard just ahead of him, ready to buy skunks. "He didn't have to ask me if I had any, because he could smell that I did." The man bought Ernie's skunks on the spot for fifty-two dollars.

Subsequently his wife got a school to teach in McIntosh County—and got forty dollars a month.

"So you see," concludes Ernie, "furs were a very important thing to us back in those days. We always had a lot of skunk. There wasn't too many people who went out and trapped skunk because of the scent and all, but once you got used to it, it just didn't seem to happen."

It may seem today like a grisly subject, but up and down the plains, den hunting for coyotes was a source of much-needed cash to rural folk of previous generations. One of my favorite family photographs shows my Grandpa Dunekeck chomping a cigar and showing off a batch of coyote pups he had taken in Barton County, Kansas. And one of my favorite literary scenes is the one after the hard winter in the middle of *Wolf Willow*, by Wallace Stegner, when the Saskatchewan ranching couple decides to stick it out on the ranch, after digging out a litter of coyotes.

The point of the enterprise, of course, was the bounties offered by the respective states and provinces. Ernie Zahn has been telling me about the importance of coyote hunting in the finances of his large German-Russian family when he was growing up in the 1920s and 1930s. I'm both rapt and wrapped, absorbed in his narrative world, reveling in the cadence of his speech.

"One of the things we would do was, the state department of agriculture was paying a bounty on coyotes, and we would do a lot of den hunting," he explains. "We knew where every den of coyotes was; these coyotes have a territory.

"In fact one Sunday we were eating dinner

Ernie Zahn's coyote diary recorded his work in predator control for U.S. Fish and Wildlife.

and a brother and I were talking about going out to find a den of coyotes. I said, you know that hole over on that east hill, right below that rock on the hill? Right there is where the den of coyotes is this year. We drove over to that pasture, drove up to that hole, and there was the den of coyotes.

"These coyote dens would have anywhere from five to fifteen pups per den. The department of agriculture was paying three dollars bounty on pups, five dollars on adults.

So if we could find a den with ten or twelve pups, this was a pretty big check for us." Especially considering that a farm-hand in those days might receive fifteen dollars a month and found, country school teachers thirty a month, likely in scrip.

"One spring," Ernie recalls, "we had 127 pups we turned in for bounty."

Just after Ernie got married, he and his wife bought a 200-acre farm for taxes, making a deal with the county to pay the taxes in installments. About the same time, he and his brothers went to South Dakota and bought a pair of greyhounds for hunting fox and coyote. "I never did tell my wife how much we paid for them greyhounds," Ernie confesses. "We paid $125 for the pair."

A few days later they saddled horses, took the dogs out, and pretty soon jumped a fox, which the hounds easily ran down. Then another fox, which the hounds also dispatched. Then a third fox, and this time the dogs ran a little, then gave up the pursuit. "They were just wore out, because we had ridden about ten miles trailing the dogs," Ernie explains.

So the boys cut a shaft from a local grove, attached it to a little two-wheel trailer, and prepared to hitch two horses to it. Onto the trailer they mounted a high box. "We filled the lower half of this box with straw, and then we put the hounds in. We would transport them from one place to another, and they would be resting and sleeping."

This worked well. The horses even got into the hunting spirit, perking up and lunging in pursuit when a fox would bolt from cover. That alerted the hounds to hop out and do their work.

"That winter," Ernie recalls with satisfaction, "we caught enough fox that I paid up the tax contract to the county in full. We had this 200-acre farm all our own."

"These potholes and wetlands, to a lot of people they were a big nuisance," observes Ernie Zahn, "but to us, they were one of the most valuable assets we had."

Now retired in Velva, Ernie grew up in a large German-Russian family in Dickey County, and during the 1920s to 1940s, they did quite a bit of living off the land—and the potholes and sloughs that covered the land.

"Trapping was the most profitable thing we did, other than the livestock on the farm," he says. "The drought ended, the potholes filled up, and we got mink, muskrat, and weasel. We'd put traplines out. We each had a riding horse, and we'd saddle up in the morning and check our trapline. We'd have traplines fifteen, eighteen, twenty miles long. We'd have two traplines, one day we'd run one, the next day the other. There was five of us boys. Four would be out trapping, while one would be taking care of the livestock. Some years we had four, five, six hundred muskrat."

Muskrat trapping was cold, hard work. Ernie explains, "You set your traps, and within hours you probably had muskrats in the traps." Hence the continual round of running the line. Too, "Muskrat was the number one food of mink," he says. "If you had a good supply of muskrat, then you had a good supply of mink.

"Us boys used different methods from most people. We used a lot of dogs in trapping mink. If it wasn't too tough, the dog was trained to go where the mink was, and in fifteen or twenty minutes of digging we already had the mink." If the mink couldn't be dug out, then they set traps.

"I remember one time I had my trapline, and we were getting ready to have Thanksgiving dinner," Ernie recalls. "It turned out snowy and blustery. The wife had cooked Thanksgiving dinner and nobody came. I said, I'm going out to check some traps."

It turned out to be a day of thanks after all. "The first mink trap I checked I had a beautiful male mink in the trap. The second trap, another mink. That night when I come home, I had seven mink. It was after dark when I got home, and my wife was concerned I might have fallen through the ice and couldn't get out. But those mink brought from fifteen to thirty-five dollars apiece. My seven mink in one day stood as our record for a number of years."

Now, the sort of life that Ernie Zahn describes in the middle of North Dakota two generations ago is, to paraphrase a great writer, a foreign country to most of us. Like many people my age I have an intense interest in traditional ways of working and providing–the knowledge of gardening and food preservation that the women of the plains devised, practiced, and perpetuated, the knowledge of crop and animal husbandry that people on the plains worked out in order to make a living from this place. What Ernie talks about, though, is a step removed from all that. He is talking about people in mid-twentieth century harvesting a substantial part of their sustenance and livelihood from fish, game, and furbearers.

And this way of life is in the recollections and life experience of people who will see the dawn of the twenty-first century.

There sometimes exist in the same country generations that are so far apart in their life experience that unless they become personally acquainted, they cannot possibly imagine one another's life experiences. People from Minneapolis or Seattle drive though the Dakotas, and they cannot understand why there are all those billboards damning animal rights and defending trapping as a way of life. Those same people have neighbors, however, born and raised on the northern plains, who know exactly where those sentiments come from. They come from the survival instincts of plains folk.

One fall along about 1940 Ernie Zahn and his brother were mowing weeds with a team and horse mower for the highway department along Highway 56 south of Kulm, North Dakota. They stopped by a slough, gave the horses some oats, ate their lunch, and rested a bit. A car stopped, and it was full of hunters.

These fellows wanted to know where they might find some pheasants. The Zahn boys were always on the lookout for any way to make a buck. So they said sure, we know where you can find some birds, but it's hard to tell you where—come up to our farm on the highway Saturday morning, and we'll take you out.

That Saturday morning the two boys were up early and impatient. "We walked down to the pasture to see if we could get any ducks," Ernie relates. "We got to a pothole and there was quite a bunch of ducks on there. We pulled a sneak on them and fired into them, and we each had our limit of mallards. And wouldn't you know it, every one was a big greenhead."

When they got back to the house, the carload of hunters pulled in from Ellendale, where they had been staying at the hotel. Ernie recalls, "We came up from the pasture, each us carrying these four nice big greenheads, and them guys just went wild. They didn't care anymore if they got any pheasants, but they wanted us to show them where they could get some of them ducks."

The hunters all got their limits of drakes that day, too. "That evening when they went into their hotel at Ellendale, they walked into the lobby with their ducks hanging across the front and back of their hunting coats, and the people were amazed. They wanted to know where and how they hunted, but they wouldn't tell, because they wanted us as their guides as long as they were there. After that, though, they did tell."

And thus the Zahn boys were launched on a career as hunting guides for out-of-state sportsmen. One problem, though, was rationing of ammunition during the war. "It was almost impossible to buy ammunition or gas," Ernie says. "We had these out-of-state hunters call us, saying they would come up by train. They would ship the ammunition to the hotel to be there when they came up. We couldn't even buy it here, but there was more than they or we could shoot up."

Guiding hunters turned into a lucrative sideline in several ways. "The pheasants, ducks, and geese were plentiful," Ernie reminisces. "The potholes were full." He recruited his mother- and father-in-law to clean birds for a price. "They were busy every afternoon and evening, sometimes practically working all night, to process the game. They would save the down feathers, and this down was worth a lot of money."

One day Ernie was supposed to take out a group of hunters, but it turned out too cold and blustery to hunt, so he took them up to the house for lunch. It being Sunday, has wife was gone to church and visiting relatives. After lunch the men got to playing gin rummy, and as you might guess, they left a certain amount of clutter around the house. Ernie was pretty worried about what his wife would say—until he noticed the fellows also had left behind four $20 bills.

"I want to say a word about the nonresident hunters," Ernie closes the story of his exploits as hunting guide. "On average, they were the best and most courteous and law-abiding citizens I ever took out. They were careful how they handled themselves when they were our guests."

If old Ernie's eyes were a little better, I'd sure try to recruit him to spend a little time down around his home country next fall.

13. Jerry-Built Contraptions

One bright day we were driving down a plains highway when I pointed out the window into a pasture and said to my wife, "Look at that beautiful homemade creep feeder." She thought about that for a minute and then asked, "Why would they want to feed them?" I can't always tell when she's serious.

It reminded me of this when, in a pasture just northeast of Medina, North Dakota, adjacent to the Medina I-94 exit, I espied a highly unusual creep feeder. Now, for the benefit of readers who are not cattle people, I'd better say just what a creep feeder is.

A creep feeder is a feed bunk or self-feeder enclosed within a barrier of some kind. The barrier allows calves up to a certain size to get through to the grain in the feeder, but it excludes the cows. The reason for having a creep feeder is to let your calves get good early growth on grain without wasting feed on your cows.

At Bailey's or the Bluestem or Wheeler's or Tractor Supply or some other farm and ranch supply store, depending on where you happen to live and work on the plains, you can buy a factory-made creep feeder, generally comprising a steel self-feeder and steel rails enclosing it. Still, though, some people make their own.

I got interested in this when I was prowling around the Flint Hills of Kansas and studying county extension records. Creep feeders, if you think about it, are indicators of land use and ranching operations. Where there are no creep feeders in the pastures, you're probably in range used for transient grazing. Where you see creep feeders, people are keeping cowherds.

In the Flint Hills during the 1930s, county agents were trying to get ranchers to ease up on transient grazing and to implement what they called the "Bluestem system"– keeping cows, creep feeding the calves, finishing them on the place, and marketing them as baby beef. One of my favorite old photos (1925) is of Elisha Stout of Chase County, Kansas, decked out in his three-piece suit, posing by his portable creep feeder while the county agent took his picture.

If you start to take an interest in pasture furniture, you notice that creep feeders usually appear along with other items–groupings sort of like your sofa, loveseat, and coffee table. Along with creep feeders you usually see windmills, mineral block boxes, and cattle oilers. One-stop shopping for your cows.

The early history of creep feeding is hard to trace. A standard textbook called *Feeds and Feeding: A Handbook for the Student and Stockman* went through many editions, beginning in 1898. The first reference to creep feeding appears in the 15th edition, 1915. A reference librarian at the National Agricultural Library, Wayne Olson, helped me out with an earlier

Creep feeder made from a hay stacker, near Medina, North Dakota.

reference, this one to creep feeding of lambs, in the *Journal of the Royal Agricultural Society*, 1845.

Getting back to Medina—this particular creep was a recycled hay stacker. Inside was a garden-variety self-feeder, but someone had the idea of enclosing it with the iron stacker frame, making a nice, roomy enclosure in which the calves could feed.

That someone was Duane Trautman, whom I called up and asked about it. Or maybe it was his father-in-law. They had a creep made of pipe around the feeder, but the calves kept swinging their rear ends around and busting it—"They just needed more room," Duane says. So they brought in the stacker.

Cows and calves go into this particular pasture about 15 June and out with weaning at the end of September. Calves up to 600 pounds can get into the feeder. Pretty good idea, Duane.

There it was, a wonderfully jerry-built contraption on an abandoned farmstead, a little bit of folk genius few people today recognize. Coming back from a grouse-hunting expedition, I spotted a homemade merry-go-round windmill.

Maybe you've seen one, but don't know what to call it. I'm borrowing my terms from that pioneering scholar of windmills, Erwin Hinckley Barbour, who published *The Homemade Windmills of Nebraska* in 1899. A merry-go-round (I'm going to say MGR for short) windmill is one where the wind-catchers turn on arms in a horizontal plane around a vertical shaft.

Years ago I spotted a dandy MGR windmill along Interstate 35 near Arkansas City, Kansas. That one was built from junk in 1937. Key parts were 55-gallon drums cut in half lengthways to serve as wind-catchers and the differential and rear axle of a Model T Ford.

This new old MGR is similar, and it's located a few miles south of the Streeter, North Dakota, exit off Interstate 94. Six half-drums mounted on 2x2 arms sit atop a wooden tower and turn a vertical shaft. The shaft runs down to the differential salvaged from some vehicle–I couldn't identify it. The wheels on the rear axle protrude out to each side, and the north wheel is connected to a pitman. That converts circular to reciprocal motion and powers the pump.

The corner legs of the tower are 4x4s, with bracing of 2-inch lumber, and with a ladder of 1-inch going up the east side.

The neighbors said, if I wanted to find out about it, call Herb Reister in Medina. It turns out the place is in an estate to which his wife, Esther, is a party along with her brother-in-law and sister-in-law. Esther and Herb gave me some background over the telephone.

The MGR was built by Gottlieb Graf, who with his wife Emma (Stolz) Graf lived and kept a small herd of grade cows on the place. Wife and husband, although born in America, were both of German-Russian stock, and I suspect not inclined to throw money around frivolously. Hence Gottlieb's homemade windmill. Neither Esther nor Herb has an idea where he got the idea for the design, but MGRs were common in Nebraska a century ago, and this is the second one I've found using oil drums and an automotive differential.

Gottlieb Graf died in about 1970, and the windmill hasn't been used since–although Herb says, "It would work to this day yet, if it was taken care of." Esther says it dates from her girlhood on the farm, but in order to date it more precisely, I'm going to have to get someone to identify that differential for me.

It was one of those wild hairs. Coming home from Montana, I decided to go looking for cable cars. In North Dakota. Obviously not cable cars of the San Francisco sort.

I'm talking about platform-cars that hang attached to pulleys on cables strung across the Little Missouri River, a little stream that lies at the bottom of a big valley running through the hills and badlands of far western North Dakota.

These precarious, homemade conveyances are used in places far from any bridge to carry people and goods across the river when the water is too high to ford.

The most famous of these is the Kruger cable car, not far north of the South Unit of Theodore Roosevelt National Park. With a good map of the Little Missouri National Grassland, I made my way to the site, pulling up on the east side of the river.

The Kruger cable car crosses the Little Missouri River on cables.

The frame of the rectangular car is of angle iron, the floor steel mesh. There is a plank seat on each end. A pair of auto wheel rims on each side ride the two half-inch steel cables that stretch across the river. A gas engine belted to a shaft turns one pair of wheels for motive power in crossing.

To come back you have to loosen the belt and reverse the drive.

The car is pretty stable on the twin cables, but that was not much comfort to my Labrador retriever, forced to sit on the swaying car and pose for the camera. After taking photos we descended the steep bank and waded, thigh-deep in cool cappuccino, unforgiving rocks on bare feet, toward the ranch on the west side. This is the place that used to be known as the Bellows Ranch.

Kermit and Cassie Kruger, owners since 1970, weren't home that day, but I got them on the telephone to ask about the story of the cable car. It seems Kermit and some neighbors built it in 1971, using a cut-down Javelin auto body for the original car. Three years or so ago they replaced the Javelin with the angle-iron-and-mesh car. They use the cable car about half the year, fording the rest of the time.

"The biggest need was school," Kermit answers in response to my question, Why? When the Kruger kids started school, at what was known as the Meyer school, it was on the east side of the river. The teacher and the Krugers lived on the west side. The teacher would ride horseback to the Kruger yard each morning and take the cable car across the river with the kids. After a couple of years they moved the school into a mobile unit on the Krugers' side.

The Krugers still have foster kids on the place, and today they use the cable car to catch a school bus on the east side to grade school in Medora or high school in Belfield. How do they like it, I asked. "It's a big thrill for them," Kermit says.

Occasionally too big a thrill. One day in about 1975 the
river was running bank full. Kermit was away, attending his
brother's wedding. Cassie and a Kruger son were aboard the
cable car in mid-river when it flipped and dipped, putting
them into the river. Fortunately, the force of the water held
them into their seats. It was hard to get out, but they did,
and they walked the twisted cables to shore. "We almost
met our maker," Cassie recalls.

Recently Kermit made a few improvements, including
a transmission on the engine, so you no longer have to
reverse the drive manually.

Crossing the river sitting high on a cable car would be
fun, I think. The first couple of times. This is one of those
inconveniences, however picturesque, that go with living
in a beautiful, barely accessible place on the plains.

I know there has been a lot of controversy about
petroleum development in the Little Missouri National
Grassland, but if you're sort of lost, looking for a cable car
across the Little Missouri River, then you have reason to
be thankful for pump jacks and tank yards. Every yard has
a little sign on the gate giving its legal description.

Having taken a look at the Kruger cable car crossing
the Little Missouri not far north of the Theodore
Roosevelt National Park, I headed downriver in search of
another, at the Tescher (previously known as the 4 Bar)
Ranch. There were some low-water crossings and twists
and turns en route, but I finally got down off the bluffs and
onto the bottom and made my way to the east bank of the
river. Here was the cable car platform, and the car was across
the river at the Tescher place on the high west bank.

So it was back into the muddy water across a rocky, swift-running ford. Nobody home at the ranch, so I just had a quick look at the little cable car.

The car hangs from two pulley wheels that ride atop a single steel cable stretched some 300 feet across the river. The car comes in at ground level on the ranch side, but running level across, it arrives at a platform twenty feet off the ground on the east side. The frame of the car is flat iron, the bottom and two sides (it's open front and back) one-inch lumber.

I stepped gingerly on, bounced a little, and it was a wobbly thing. I wondered how you propelled it and kept it balanced.

That's what I asked Troy Tescher, who grew up on the place. He said, "You unhook the chain, give it a push, and jump on, and it will go out half or two-thirds of the way." Then, kneeling, you pull yourself hand over hand on the cable.

Troy said talk to his dad, Jim, about the cable car, and so I did. He says he and Loretta moved to the ranch in 1952, raised their five kids there, and moved off in 1991. Now they live on another ranch on Beaver Creek northeast of Beach.

The cable car was in place when the Teschers moved onto the place on the Little Missouri. It goes back at least into the 1940s and maybe the 1930s. If someone knows the earlier history of it, I'd be happy to hear.

The oldest Tescher boy, Gary, was the first in the family to use the cable car to go to school, which was four and a half miles on from the east end of the cable car. When the river was low, he forded it horseback. When a storm came on, he stayed over with the teacher or other folks on the east side.

Jim says he's heard the story of a fellow who, finding the cable car on the wrong side of high water when he wanted to cross, hung from the cable and crossed the river hand over hand. He also recalls the time he and two other guys were coming across from the east side, the cable was sagging a little, and they got stuck in the middle, dipping into the water with big old logs coming downstream at them. They made their way back to the east side and decided to try again later.

For years the mail came just twice a week from Medora, and it was delivered to the cable car platform on the east bank. The Teschers had to pull across to get their mail. "That baby was tough pulling," Jim allows, "and if there was a wind it was tougher."

The last new cable was put on in 1950 or so. Sometime in the late 1970s they rebuilt the car and put new pulleys on it, and although it isn't much used, it's serviceable. "We've hauled hay across on it, we've hauled cake, we even took a fanning mill across on it," says Jim, and he has taken as many as four other people across on it. That must have taken some careful balancing, and perhaps a little prayer.

14. It Makes the Place Survive

Marj Deibert said to check out Hunter's Table and Tavern, in Rhame, western Bowman County, North Dakota. She's a custom harvester from Hoxie, Kansas, and her outfit makes Hunter's a port of call. So when I was in the vicinity for some extension work, I stopped to see the place and meet the owners, Karen and Wayne Miller.

The first memorable thing about Hunter's is its appearance. A low, slant-roofed structure lurking behind the Cenex station south of Highway 13, the building ought to be unobtrusive, except for its peculiarities. It was built by Rae and Rob Getz in 1982-83 by the method known as cordwood masonry.

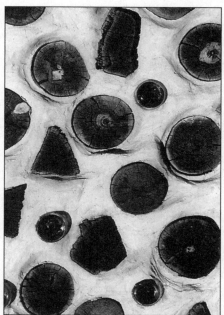

Cordwood masonry wall of Hunter's Table and Tavern, Rhame, North

Rob cut stacks of cedar from fire-killed stands and from used fenceposts. Rae supervised an all-woman construction crew on the site. The method was to lay, atop a concrete foundation and floor, walls of 16-

inch-length logs stacked like cordwood and joined with concrete–resulting in sturdy, 16-inch-thick walls with a remarkable mottled facade. Here and there, too, they used a whiskey bottle in place of a log.

The roof is cedar beams, tongue-and-groove paneling on the beams, then black plastic, then a foot of flax straw, and finally, a layer of red scoria rock. Thistles grow from the roof now, like they did from old sod houses.

The interior is made the more rustic by the two central, stone fireplaces. On the bar side, antlers and mounted heads carry through the "Hunter's" motif.

Besides its structural interest, the place has good food. The fare is plain–chicken, steaks, chicken fried steaks, and so on–but the meat is cut on the premises, the potatoes are real, the chicken fried steak is breaded thick and brown (although it needs some white gravy, both for my taste and for the sake of all the Oklahoma roughnecks who come in). Indian taco night on Thursday always draws a crowd. "Once they stop here, they come back," Karen Miller says.

The Millers bought Hunter's in 1987. They ran it themselves, then leased it, and when I got there, Karen was pretty much running it again. (Wayne is more occupied with the family ranch, 22 miles south. He also is part of a western singing group, the Sons of the Wagoneers.) Business is better than ever. Farmers and ranchers drive in, basketball fans stop by, the oil business has picked up again.

And that brings me to the third reason why Hunter's is so remarkable. I heard it said of Hunter's and its role in Rhame, "It makes the place survive." There are the coffee clatches, men's and women's, morning and afternoon. A young crowd makes the bar side, managed by Don

Arithson, its hangout. Hunters in fall, tourists in summer join the local and working folk.

"It makes the place survive"—as a center of local community, as an outpost for travelers. Long may it be so.

It was so at least a few years later when I returned to Bowman County with Lotte to commence the Historic Architectural Survey of Bowman County—work done under contract with the State Historical Society of North Dakota. We documented 252 sites, took more than a thousand photographs, and drove every section road or lease road in the county.

Early in the survey, as we worked the east half of the county, Scranton Pizza developed into our main port of call. Later, as we worked the west half of the county, we shifted over to the Table and Tavern, which we found under new but competent management. Of an evening, after ten or twelve hours of field work and supper and a beer or two at Hunter's, I would walk out into the dusk singing (in loose paraphrase of the old cowboy standard, "Rye Whiskey"),

> If you're looking for a hot time gonna find one
>   right here
> When the roughnecks and the cowhands come in
>   for a beer.
> I'll eat when I'm hungry, drink when I'm dry,
> At the Table and Tavern I'll live 'til I die.
> The walls are of cordwood and mortar well laid;
> With a bottle of whiskey the workmen were paid.
> The roof is of scoria rock laid on plank
> And the tumbleweeds growing upon it are rank.

In any good bookstore, you find coffee-table books devoted to barns. We like barns because they are monumental anachronisms. They have lost utility in the modern agricultural landscape. The milking stanchions are rusted shut, and it's hard to put big round bales in the loft.

While we revere barns in general, I think we are conceited in our tastes about them. The barns we respect are the ones that fit certain ideals of design and craftsmanship tracing back to some such hearth as Pennsylvania. We see a bank barn with a threshing floor and maybe even a hex on the door, and we get all gooey.

Use of native materials also scores high in regard for barns. I remember working on the nomination of the Rogler Ranch in Chase County, Kansas, for the National Register of Historic Places, and an important feature in the nomination was the barn. No one could argue the barn was not historic, because the beams were hewn from the nearby Cottonwood River bottom. Up the road at the new Tallgrass Prairie National Preserve, the old Z Bar or Spring Creek Ranch, a key attraction is the massive barn. This is a great barn by both its history and its design, but a large element of its appeal is that it is constructed of good old Flint Hills limestone.

What make these barns great, however, are things not to be found in most parts of the plains–quality timber and building stone. What about the great expanses of the Great Plains without such assets? This country is spangled with barns, too, that have to be met on their own terms. If you grew up on a farm or ranch in the Great Plains, as I did in central Kansas, then I'll bet the barn on your place did not incorporate hewn timbers or native stone.

I'll bet it was more like the many barns we documented for the state historical society in Bowman County. These were all twentieth-century barns built after the railroad had arrived. They were constructed of milled lumber and put on foundations of concrete.

Yet they are magnificent in the open landscape, and various in their functions and design. The classic barn in this part of the country had a gambrel roof—what local people call a "hip roof," but that's really something else. A gambrel roof was intended to maximize loft space. An arch roof achieved much the same purpose and is, I think, even more elegant, but arch roofs are less common.

We were particularly impressed with the gambrel-roof barn of a woman named Vivian Davis. She's a native of the area and a retired schoolteacher who taught in military schools all over the world, then inherited the family farm and moved back. She has put that big loft to use by holding barn dances. The greatest public service given by her barn, though, is just standing there. That splendid red barn is the most prominent landmark in the eastern half of a large county.

And then there are the sheep barns, something new to our experience. I'm told that ventilation is quite important in a lambing building, and so the great old sheep barns have distinctive monitor roofs. A monitor roof-line has low flanks with roof faces sloping up to a taller central section, where the upper walls rise vertically again and are capped by a narrow gable. Superior ventilation is achieved by windows in this upper part. The roof-line also makes sheep barns distinguishable from a distance.

These barns deserve our respect. In the level and rolling and sparsely populated landscapes of the plains, they are like grand cathedrals.

Scanning the Great Plains today, we can easily be misled to think that this is a land of wheat and cattle and always has been. No doubt our ancestors who settled the country did expect to make good money from the major commodities, but they also had other ideas. They believed in the ideal of the diversified family farm–the old "cow, sow, and hen" idea. The proof of their belief is there, materially, when you walk about old farmsteads.

Chicken houses, for instance. In the past few years historians of rural women have been pointing out through reference to census materials and diaries how important it was that women kept farm flocks and brought in egg money. I'd like to point to another piece of evidence of the importance of hens–the material and technique spent on chicken houses.

This is something I became aware of through research in my native state of Kansas, especially extension reports of the 1920s and 1930s. To begin with, though, I remember that my grandparents had a substantial chicken house on the farm where I grew up in Barton County. It was a long building with lots of windows on the long wall facing east. The laying boxes ran the length of a room on this east side from one end to the other. Back of this room was a roosting chamber, and in one corner a granary. On top the chicken house, although I never would have known to call it this at the time, was a semi-monitor roof.

Now getting into those extension reports, I was amazed at all the attention lavished on chickens. You might think this was just one of those extension ideas that maybe the farm folk themselves were dubious about, but no–the photos show that people were just flocking to demonstrations of how to cull the flock, how to make capons, how to kill rats in the chicken house, and so on.

As to housing the flock, the great concerns were hygienic. Ventilation was important, and also the idea arrived in the 1920s that in order to minimize disease—chickens die if you just look at them hard—you should have chicken houses on skids and move them around. I remember one county agent pasted in his report a photo of a smiling woman in an apron next to her portable chicken house with the caption, "It pays to raise poultry on clean ground."

After spending a summer surveying farm buildings in Bowman County, North Dakota, I can tell you, around here portability was not a priority. The big problem was keeping a flock alive, and preferably laying, through a long, cold winter.

The chicken houses show how they did it. First, build low, exposing as little external wall as possible to the elements. Second, put a bank of windows on the south wall, so as to gather as much solar warmth and light as possible. And third, build tight.

Courtesy State Historical Society of North Dakota.

Stucco chicken houses (such as this one in Bowman County) helped keep hens alive and laying on the northern plains.

Quite a few of these northern chicken houses were given exteriors of stucco, so as to make them tighter and better insulated. This also made them remarkably attractive buildings.

And distinctive, too, because of their design. The classic chicken house of the northern plains has what is called a saltbox roof, meaning one of the long walls is taller than its opposite, and thus one face of the roof extends longer and lower than the other. The taller wall, with windows, is on the south side.

So there was a time when people made chickens a priority on farms of the plains. I can also tell you, though, that in the course of our survey of farm buildings in 1997, in a whole county, we found exactly two chicken houses occupied by flocks.

We take them for granted, these homely little buildings strewn about our farmsteads and shelterbelts, but they are the architectural signature of wheat farming on the northern plains. I'm talking about granaries.

If you've lived all your life here, you may not realize how distinct a signature this is. I spent most of my life in the winter wheat country of the southern plains and then began traveling the northern plains extensively in my work, and granaries were one of the things I noticed. For a variety of reasons having to do both with environment and with the infrastructure of grain marketing, on-farm storage of grain has been historically much more prevalent in the north.

Wheat culture was booming early in this century, when railroads opened so much of the northern plains to settlement, and so among the first buildings erected on new farmsteads were granaries—wooden ones. Generally they were set atop concrete piers (not full foundations) that lifted them 18 inches or so off the ground.

The walls were upright studs covered with horizontal siding. The roofs usually were low gables—occasionally shed roofs in the ruder ones—covered with wood shingles. The roofs generally had no eaves; they cut off flush with the wall.

The typical granary of this early heyday of wheat culture was of boxy dimensions, some 12 by 16 feet. It had a grain compartment in each end. Grain was deposited through square ports high under the gables, or sometimes in the roof. A door in the middle of one of the longer sides provided access to a central interior alley between the compartments, where grain was removed.

That's the basic form, but some people went beyond the basic. More ambitious wheat farmers built longer granaries with more compartments and thus more doors for access to them. This also meant the grain had to be put in through the roof.

The resurgence of wheat culture in the 1940s brought about construction of some even more impressive granaries, of drive-through design. There would be a line of grain compartments along either long wall, rolling doors on each end, and an alley down the middle for trucks.

Most of what I say here is based on research and field work in Bowman County. The most outstanding granary we found in that survey was one in the north part of the county that fit this 1940s description. It was particularly striking because of its monitor roof.

Most granaries, though, as I say, are much more humble. In fact by the time that outstanding wooden granary was built, almost everyone else had ceased building wooden ones and commenced buying round steel ones. The first of these date from the 1930s. We found several in Bowman County bearing a stenciled legend, "Ever Normal Granary," and a number. This indicates they were used to seal wheat under the New Deal farm program.

Another important fact about granaries is that they are portable, not only the new metal ones but also the old wooden ones. As everybody knows, there are a lot fewer farms today than there were when the country was settled up. And granaries were too useful just to leave them strewn about the abandoned farms. People hauled them home and arranged them around their own yards and shelterbelts, resulting in regular colonies of granaries.

This sort of portable material of history doesn't get much respect, but it ought to. For better or worse, the welfare of our part of the country has been inextricably tied to wheat, and the granaries grouped on our surviving farms are the symbol of it.

The profound prairie essayist John Ingalls of Kansas wrote, "Grass is the forgiveness of nature." Whatever carnage people might wreak upon the land, he said, grass eventually would cover and heal. If grass is the forgiveness of nature, then stucco is the forgiveness of architecture. From Texas to Saskatchewan, settlers on the Great Plains have used stucco to make their houses more livable.

Euro-Americans arriving on the plains were inclined to build houses that were not practical. (We still do, of course.) What sense did it make to erect a big Foursquare farmhouse, or a tall Gabled Front house, on the open plains, with their extremes of heat and cold and wind? Those wood-frame houses exposed way too much exterior to the elements, were not tight enough, and were hard to insulate. Even modest wood-frame houses had the same problems in degree. What could be done?

Stucco—an exterior coating of some combination of cement and sand and gravel and plaster, the mix varied—was the answer. Tack up some chicken wire, and stucco could be applied to existing walls. Better yet, it could be applied as the exterior right from the start.

Stucco was the plainsperson's answer to adobe, in compromise fashion. Builders on the plains kept their traditional architectural designs, but changed the exterior to stucco. It was not a perfect or complete adaptation to environment, but it was an improvement.

If you are at home on the plains, then when you get into country where the buildings are stucco, you feel good. I feel good traveling western Kansas and western Oklahoma and eastern Colorado, country full of stucco Bungalows with ponderous porches built during the heyday of wheat farming in the 1920s.

I felt good exploring Bowman County, North Dakota, on a survey of historic architecture for the state historical society. In this country there seemed to be a strong connection between sheep ranching and stucco.

Right now I'm looking at a selection of photographs of modest, one-story stucco ranch houses. What great buildings these are for the Great Plains! Built low in the walls and in the gables, they seem part of the rolling landscape. In a practical sense, they expose the minimum exterior wall to the elements. They are well-built and well-finished, too. None of these houses has been occupied for many years, but they stand sound and with even their exteriors intact.

On another sheep ranch, this one still in operation, we photographed the old ranch house, of stucco—that was to be expected—but there was much more. This place even had a vaulted-roofed airplane hangar of stucco, a beautiful combination of the earthy and the ethereal.

We found barns covered with stucco. Applying a stucco exterior to a barn was a considerable undertaking, but worth it, I suppose, if you cared about your livestock. Or perhaps the concern was for the milkers working in the barn, who would prefer to work in a stucco building! I noticed that those who stuccoed their barns generally only covered the ground level; the exterior of the loft was wood siding.

I'm a stucco fan. I like it on ranch houses in the Bad-lands, I like it on farmhouses in the Panhandle, I like it on the little cottages in the working-class neighborhoods of Regina.

Is there any garden scene prettier than a stand of hardy hollyhocks pastel against a whitewashed stucco wall?

15. Montana Caviar

Paddlefish are the stuff of stories. While Francisco Vasquez de Coronado was trekking across the plains and feasting on buffalo, Hernan de Soto was making his way down the Mississippi River and dining on paddlefish hauled from its backwaters. Early settlers of the interior of North America described paddlefish as wondrous monsters of two and three hundred pounds–fish stories that modern biologists do not discount, because no one today knows how big a paddlefish, left undisturbed in good habitat, can get.

Sometimes called "shovelcats," paddlefish are not catfish, but a species closely related to sturgeon. Their original range was throughout the Mississippi River basin, which meant they were found in all the rivers of the American plains. And today the most notable sport fisheries for paddlefish are in plains states.

Paddlefish have a checkered history. In some ways the works of man have hurt them, and in other ways human constructions have helped them.

A century ago, and again in recent years, paddlefish have been exploited commercially. In 1899 about 900 tons of them were taken from the Mississippi. Today there is a more modest harvest from the Tennessee River and its lakes.

As with most wildlife issues, the more important question is habitat. Paddlefish have particular requirements. They are river fish, they make upstream runs to spawn, but they like slack water. The confinement of the Mississippi and other rivers to narrow channels by levees, dredging, and other construction was disastrous for paddlefish, because it eliminated the backwaters. Likewise the construction of dams interfered with spawning by blocking upstream movements or, in some cases, by flooding spawning grounds.

On the other hand, in some cases the construction of dams created new and ideal habitat for paddlefish. The still waters of great reservoirs proved wonderfully hospitable to these peculiar fish, who fed on the freshwater equivalent of plankton. (Greg Power, of North Dakota Game and Fish, corrected my earlier misconception that paddlefish were bottom-feeders. "In fact," he explains, "they spend the better part of their life suspended in the water, always in search of something very small to eat!") Where good spawning grounds were accessible upstream from the reservoirs, paddlefish population explosions ensued.

That accounts for the healthy populations of paddlefish in the Tennessee River Valley. Closer to the plains we have Lake of the Ozarks, on the Osage River. In the 1930s, following construction of Bagnell Dam, fishermen began snagging paddlefish in river holes above the lake during spring spawning times. The subsequent construction of Truman Dam, however, flooded the spawning areas.

There persists a modest sport fishery for paddlefish in the Osage catchment, extending into eastern Kansas. The most significant fishery on the southern plains is at Chetopa, Kansas, where paddlefish coming up from Grand Lake of the Cherokees are halted by a dam across the Neosho River.

It is on the northern plains, however, where paddlefish attract the greatest attention.

So many important changes on the Great Plains flow
from the Pick-Sloan plan, the U.S. Army Corps of Engineers scheme to transform the Missouri River. Bottomland
farmers along the southern tributaries of the Missouri raised
political hell along with their corn, but they couldn't stop
the building of the dams, not even the controversial Tuttle
Puddle on the Kaw. In North Dakota the "dammed Indians"
(that's from the title of a good book on the subject) were
flooded out by Garrison Dam. Ivan Doig's fine novel,
Bucking the Sun, tells the story of the great earthen Fort Peck
Dam in Montana.

Plains folk not displaced from their homes and farms by
the new great lakes were drawn to them as recreational
magnets. Today their famous fisheries draw sportsmen from
all over the country.

An unexpected windfall from the big dams was a profusion of paddlefish. It was the same story as with the TVA
lakes, or Lake of the Ozarks, or Grand Lake of the Cherokees. The lakes flooded some spawning areas, they interfered
with upstream runs, but they also created great expanses of
slack water ideal for the maturation of paddlefish.

Today there is a flourishing paddlefish sport fishery in
the Nebraska-South Dakota boundary waters of the Missouri below Gavins Point Dam—the Yankton area. If you're
gung-ho to catch a paddlefish, though, where you want to
go is farther upstream, the fisheries above Lake Sakakawea—
at Williston, North Dakota, and Glendive, Montana.

At the latter point, on the Yellowstone River,
paddlefishing got started in the early 1900s, following
construction of a diversion dam, the Intake, for a local
irrigation district. Paddlefish running up the Yellowstone
were stopped or delayed by the Intake dam, where fisher-

man waded in and snagged them. At Glendive's Frontier
Gateway Museum I found a dandy photo, dated 1911, of
several Glendive swains showing off a catch of shovel-nose
sturgeon and two paddlefish.

In subsequent years paddlefishing on the Yellowstone
was forgotten; perhaps the population declined, or perhaps
it was just neglected. Suddenly, in 1962, paddlefish were
rediscovered. As the proprietor of the Beer Jug tavern and
tackle in Glendive recalled, "A guy came in here and took a
few cheap lures"–intending to fish for pike at the Intake.
When the fellow came back, he was pretty excited. He said,
"I caught the craziest looking fish you ever saw!" Scherger
recollected, "After that everybody went plum crazy."

For a few years the fish caught at the Intake were mainly
males of modest size, but in time there were more and more
females, much larger–60 pounds, then 80, then 90. What
was happening was that as Lake Sakakawea filled, a paddlefish population began to build. The males matured and ran
upstream earlier, at the age of perhaps ten years. The females
reached maturity later.

Fishermen flocked by the thousands to the Intake,
creating a pretty chaotic scene. The sport was exciting, but
some of the effects were ugly–such as the tons of stinking,
fly-fetching heaps of paddlefish remains left behind by
fishermen cleaning their monster catches at riverside.

Paddlefish are kin to sturgeon, remember. Lying among
the remains of those paddlefish, discarded by heedless
fishermen, were the eggs carried by the heavy female fish. A
local restauranteur looked over the mess and shook his
head, saying, "It's a shame to waste it. We're looking at
thousands of dollars here."

Montana caviar.

Heading west on 94 for Glendive, Montana, it felt like a Great Plains expedition. The speed limit was back up where it belonged, I had Andy Wilkinson and Chuck Suchy in the cassette player, and I was on my way to catch a paddle-fish.

The spring had been slow, but it was mid-June, and John Trangmoe, Mr. Paddlefish at the Glendive Chamber of Commerce, had told me the run was on. Arriving in Glendive, I was informed by the sign above the Chamber door that 850 paddlefish already had been caught. I headed over to the Beer Jug tavern and tackle ("Your Paddlefish Headquarters," the sign says) to get a license and the low-down on the fishing scene.

Then I drove northeast of town out to the Intake. The campground was well occupied, a few people were casting, and more were watching. We watched a petite young woman (estimated weight 100 pounds) battle and land a paddlefish of 85 pounds. It was a real question who was catching whom.

Next morning I headed back to the Intake. Arriving at 6:00 AM or so, I met Les Reichelt; he and Lisa operate the concessions at the paddlefishing site below the diversion dam. Les fixed me up with tackle–salt-water spinning rig, 40# line, big treble hooks, heavy weights, all rented real reasonable–ferried me across to the Joe's Island side of the Yellowstone, and pointed out what he thought was the best place to hook a big one.

No kidding. Wading into the muddy splash, I cast for about five minutes and hooked a shovel-nose sturgeon, five pounds or so. I put him back and flailed the water for another ten minutes, when I hooked something heavy.

There was no way to reel in this fish against the current. For fifteen minutes or so I just tried to contain its runs, following it downstream a bit. Then the fish tired, and the current pushed it near shore. By this time there were other fishermen on the scene. A fellow named Roger from Deadwood jumped into the river and gaffed my fish for me.

My fish was a relatively small one, a male of 36 inches and 31 pounds, which I hauled into the riverbank shade. I tagged the fish and was done fishing. It was pleasant there on Joe's Island—gallery forest of cottonwood, buffalo berry understory, boughs filled with birdsong, pelicans cruising the river.

The fishing was picking up. I heard one angler after another cry out as tender feet touched the chilly waters. Cast and jerk, cast and jerk. I saw Roger's sister Lisa, a pretty ranch woman from Belle Fourche, lean back on her tackle, and then I heard her shout, "I've got a fish! What the hell do I do now?!"

She and I shared the boat ride back to the weighing and cleaning stations on the concession side of the river. Picture-taking ensued. The Glendive Chamber had a refrigerated semi-trailer set up, where a crew managed by Carol and Bob Kuehn cleaned all fish for free—or rather, in exchange for the caviar carried by the female fish. You can't beat this deal! Who wants to clean a fish like that?

Paddlefishing the muddy waters at the Intake, Glendive, Montana, is a group thing.

"The girls pay the bills," says a smiling Bob Kuehn, deftly extracting eggs from a sixty-pound paddlefish. I had brought my fish, a smaller male, in for cleaning, and stayed around to learn about the paddlefish caviar business as practiced in Glendive, Montana.

Bob, his son Ty, and employee Todd Thompson do all the fish cleaning, up to 200 a day. (Says Todd, "You have nightmares about fish.") They remove the eggs from the females; slice off the fillets; cut away the "belly lining" and "red meat" filled with blood vessels that nobody wants to eat; put the fillets into a plastic bag; and close the bag with the Montana tag taken from the dorsal fin of the fish.

A good-size female fish yields about 14 pounds of eggs. The record from a single fish is 26.5 pounds.

The eggs, in stainless steel bowls, are passed to the women in the back room of the semi-trailer–Bob's wife Carol, their daughter Leigh Ann, and Ty's wife Erin. Bob says it takes a soft touch to screen, sort, and salt the eggs–"I can't do it," he insists.

Cleaning paddlefish (and saving roe) for the Glendive, Montana, Chamber of Commerce.

He pours me a cup of coffee, and Carol takes me around
back into the refrigerated storage unit, showing me the
plastic containers in which the caviar is stacked to age for
two weeks or so. She says it comes in varying colors–dark
gray, light gray, dark green, medium green–"but the dark
gray are the prettiest." Yes, she agrees, women are better
than men at handling tender caviar.

The Kuehn clan contracts with the Glendive Chamber
of Commerce to handle paddlefish at the Intake for "so
much a fish and a percentage of the caviar." How did this
business come about?

It took an act of the Montana legislature, in 1989.
Members of the Glendive Chamber were behind this.
They saw the sad waste of caviar, and in it an opportunity.
The new law legalized the sale (out-of-state only) of
paddlefish caviar, but gave a monopoly on such commerce
to the Glendive Chamber. It would have been unaccept-
able to let individuals trade in a product taken from game
fish; already there were problems with bootlegging of roe.
Profits from caviar sales were to fund paddlefish research
by the Department of Fish, Wildlife and Parks; to develop
recreational facilities for paddlefishing; and to fund local
community charities.

Soon after, a similar deal was struck by the Williston
Chamber of Commerce with the North Dakota legislature.

These carefully controlled operations are good things.
Fishermen benefit, of course, but there is a more important
effect. The towns of Glendive and Williston now have
powerful community stakes in this wonderful monster of the
Missouri, the paddlefish. They advocate wise and sustainable management of the resource. Should other interests–
mining interests in Montana, for instance–contemplate

actions that threaten paddlefish environment, they will
have to reckon with the folks in Glendive and Williston.
Local folk consider violators of fishing laws thieves and
report them. Fish and wildlife officials in Montana and
North Dakota find they have good friends when they work
to protect the paddlefish.

On the line is Lou Ann Engwicht, of New Salem,
North Dakota. I gather she has a remarkable family—"I raised
seventeen kids," she says—and does a lot of hunting, fishing,
and gardening. She wants to know what I know about
cleaning paddlefish. I explain what I observed in the processing trailer at Glendive. It seems she and her family went
to Williston and caught seven fish among them. They plan
on going back, and next time they intend to clean their
own fish.

As we converse, I sense that this woman knows a lot
about handling fish, game, and garden truck. She pickles
pike and catfish, nets smelt in the Heart River, knows at
least three good ways to cook paddlefish flesh. I mention
to her I have some whitetail jackrabbits around my place
that are about to pay the ultimate penalty for ring-barking
my fruit trees, and she gives me instructions on how to
cook one. It involves plenty of onions and about three
hours cooking time.

Hang up, and on to class, where a student presents me
with this. You probably heard what happened out at
Garrison Dam, right? There was some sort of problem with
the outlet, and so they had to send divers and welders down
into the lake to fix it. They worked just a little while, and
then they came out and wouldn't go back in. They were too
scared.

They said there were giant fish down there, monster paddlefish. Finally they said they would go back down only if the authorities provided a shark cage for them to work in. That's what they did then.

Heck, they should have just called Greg Power, and he could have told them the paddlefish were only looking for something "very small" to eat.

Dorothy Deethardt, we need you at our house. You are a woman undaunted by any culinary challenge. Your letter arrived at a time when I thought I was through with writing about paddlefish, but by no means through with cooking my catch.

My writings on paddlefish attracted a certain amount of interest, including inquiries about the merits of the fish on the table. This question has been the subject of debate in my own house. Personally, I found broiled paddlefish fine, and paddlefish chowder excellent. My spouse respectfully disagreed. I believe the problem was that she saw the homely fish before its flesh made its way to the table.

Getting back to Ms. Deethardt–she was a food scientist at South Dakota State University when the construction of great reservoirs on the plains was producing a boom in paddlefishing. She saw the problem taking shape as guys began snagging these behemoths from the rivers of the plains. "The unusual size of the paddlefish," she observed wryly, "has left some homemakers at a loss as to what to do with so much fish at one time." Exactly.

Hence South Dakota Agricultural Experiment Station Publication B651, *Paddlefish*. It's out of print, but Deethardt was kind enough to send me a copy from her files. Here are

instructions for filleting a paddlefish and a remarkable array
of recipes.

Some of them are orthodox–recipes for broiling, baking,
boiling, and frying the fish. There are white, almandine, and
drawn butter sauces. If you want to go farther, there are
paddlefish casserole, paddlefish pie, and paddlefish hors
d'oeuvres with chili sauce. Feeling cross-cultural? Then try a
paddlefish curry spiced with ginger, curry, turmeric, and red
pepper.

Evidently paddlefish were insufficient challenge for
Deethardt, because she also tackled the carp issue. With
carp cookery we are truly entering the culinary frontier–as
people see things around here. Of course, as Deethardt
points out, carp are cultivated and prized in most other parts
of the world, and the quality of their flesh depends on the
quality of the water they inhabit. With the reservoirs of the
plains producing great expanses of good water habitat, she
reasoned, it was time for carp to make a culinary statement
in the region.

That statement is South Dakota Agricultural Experiment Station Publication B646, *Crafty Carp Cookery*. You
can read the title two ways, but I think the "crafty" part
refers to the cookery, not the carp.

Again, here are instructions for filleting the fish, including how to remove the objectionable dark flesh along the
flank. Here are the customary modes of cooking. And here,
even more so than with the paddlefish, are the amazing
recipes.

A partial catalog: carp chowder, carp sausage, carp
salami, carp and potato pancakes, carp and bulgur pudding,
carp loaf (three versions), carp lasagna, carp croquettes, carp
omelet, and carp souffle.

Now the salad section, and I am not making any of this up: carp-banana salad, carp apple sandwich spread, and carp cranberry mold. I mean it, carp Jell-O! All that's missing here is glorified carp-and-rice.

Because people on the northern plains do quite a bit of pickling of fish, both the paddlefish and the carp bulletins give instructions for canning and pickling the fish.

Thank you, Dorothy Deethardt. You have given me renewed courage—and made me seem conservative.

16. Plum Butter

"Plum butter" is the answer. The question is, What's the best thing to do with the native plums I picked out in the shelterbelt?

A little disquisition about plums of the plains: There are two kinds common. On the southern plains we have *Prunus angustifolia*, commonly called sandhill plum, sometimes called Chickasaw plum. These are the plums so admired by Coronado's soldiers in 1541. The bushes are short, three to eight feet tall, they grow in pasture thickets, and the plums are bright red. Sandhill plums are without peer for jelly, which is simply iridescent.

On the northern plains we have *Prunus americana*, the common native plum, often planted as an under-story in shelterbelts. (In fact old folks down in Kansas, where I grew up, called these "shelterbelt plums" when they were introduced from the north with the shelterbelt projects of the 1930s, distinguishing them from the sandhill plums.) They grow a bit taller than sandhill plums, and the fruit when ripe ranges from yellow to crimson. These shelterbelt plums make good jelly, but it isn't as pretty as sandhill plum jelly. On the other hand, their yellow flesh is mild and juicy, much better than that of sandhill plums. The only drawback is that their skins are rather bitter.

The shelterbelt plums come ripe at summer's end or autumn's beginning. I have a few little trees grown from suckers dug out of the neighbor's shelterbelt, and bless their hearts, they are among the few perennial things that have bounced back well after being inundated for a couple of weeks in the Big Water of 1997. About Memorial Day they filled with pale, scenty blossoms, and plenty of fruit followed. They give me a couple of buckets of beautiful fruit to make into plum butter. Here's the regime.

First you have to press out the pulp. You do the plums in lots to fit your colander, heating them with just a little water on the stove, stirring them up now and then, until about half of them burst.

Now, this part is important. When you're pressing the plums through the colander, take it easy with that pestle. You don't want to be bruising and pulverizing those bitter skins, because if you do, that taste will come right through to your plum butter. These plums pulp out easily, anyway. The product looks a lot like applesauce.

Plum butter is basically plum pulp and sugar cooked down to the consistency of a spread. How much sugar depends on your fruit and your tastes, but shelterbelt plums are not very tart, and so as a rule of thumb—about two cups of sugar to three cups of pulp. The only spice I add is cinnamon, but maybe you're more creative than that. You can do the cooking stove-top on low heat; I use a crock-pot and let it simmer all day.

Plum butter can be canned and processed, or frozen, or used and given away fresh. Now we're getting to my favorite part of the story, which is use.

Plum butter does not go with wimpy white breads. I wouldn't use it with biscuits, either. Biscuits require something more delicate, like say rose-hip jelly. Plum butter is the spread for your whole wheat breads, nutty crunchy breads, toasted. It might even be spread on such hearty toast as the under-story for a slab of fried oatmeal sausage.

There is one use even better for plum butter, so good I
hesitate to tell it, but for the sake of quality of regional life,
I will: kolaches. You know, those Bohemian pastries Chuck
Suchy sings about. Spread out your dough, cut your circles,
make the little hole with your thumb, and fill it with plum
butter. After baking, sprinkle with powdered sugar. Then get
out of the way.

The northern plains are not a region famed for cuisine.
Like any cultural region, it has strong folkways of food, and
like any physical region, it has distinctive local staples, but
people here have not built on those traditions and materials
to create a notable cuisine.

It's about time. That's why at the West Fargo Branch
Station for Applied Alternative Horticulture we're smoking
up the kitchen night and day. Focus of experiments in the
1998 season: red currants.

Grow what grows is our motto, and gooseberries and
currants love this latitude. The standard variety for red
currants in these parts is Red Lake; that's what we raise.
They bear like the dickens, and what a beautiful fruit!

The trouble is most people don't know what to do with
all the fruit. Jelly, of course, with great color and a taste
just right for biscuits. (Try a biscuit, butter, currant jelly,
and slice of ham sandwich.) Then there's syrup, which you
can dribble into a glass of club soda for a great cooler. We
make a light syrup—about three cups sugar to five cups juice.

The currant event of the summer, though, was when we
started using red currant syrup on meats. This was a logical
development, since currant jelly often is paired with lamb or
game. The syrup, through, is more adaptable. Just follow our
lab manual.

Experiment #1: CCC on the grill. The C's are cilantro, currant syrup, and chicken. First saute some fresh foliage of cilantro, then add some syrup and bring it to a boil. That's your sauce. Slice a couple of breasts off one of those chunky Hutterite chickens and grill them slow, drowning them in the sauce. Remember you read about it here.

Experiment #2: chops on the grill, two variations—pork and lamb. For the pork, rub the chops with whatever seasonings you fancy. (I like a Cajun mix myself.) Then grill them fast, basting with currant syrup. Hit them one last time with syrup, close the grill, cut the heat, and let them steam juicy. For the lamb, make a sauce in a pan, like with the cilantro above, but use rosemary. Or maybe marjoram. Finish them on the grill like the pork.

Experiment #3: another CCC, this one on the stovetop, and this time the second C stands for chiles. Also you need some garlic, which doesn't start with C, but cloves does, so there you go. Begin with a little olive oil in a pan. Saute some cloves of garlic on low heat, like you do with garlic. Add some chopped green chiles and turn the heat up to medium. Then put in a couple of those chunky chicken breasts, dredged in flour if you like, and brown them. Add a cup of red currant syrup and simmer with no lid, so that the sauce becomes a dark reserve. Serve with rice or, better, couscous. (I wonder when the local pasta makers are going to start making couscous? Wouldn't you like to see a bumper sticker, "Eat North Dakota Couscous?")

This chicken with garlic-chile-currant sauce is as good as it gets. It's sweet and hot and altogether sensual. It's too bad partridge numbers are down on the plains, because I have a feeling you could do wonderful things pairing a currant sauce with the delicate, pale flesh of partridge. And could any pairing better represent the potential of a regional cuisine?

This adaptation of currant syrup to use with savory foods got me thinking of possibilities for that favorite of our household, plum butter. We've made some remarkable breakthroughs with plum butter, too, particularly in the area of the barbeque grill. Once again, here's the lab manual.

Experiment #1: plum butter and mustard sauce. Maybe you've made a honey-mustard sauce for pork. Do the same thing, only use plum butter instead of honey. Rub the chops with whatever seasonings you like–maybe include some sage–and use the plum-butter mustard sauce liberally. After

the final application cover the grill, turn off the heat, and let the plum flavor steam into the chops.

Experiment #2: plum butter and chile sauce. You're on your own as to proportions here, but the point is to mix the plum butter with good red chile powder, and probably some garlic, either fresh or powder. Add just a little tomato sauce, and you've got a barbeque sauce like nobody else's, great on pork or chicken.

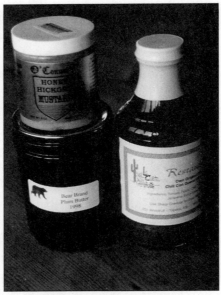

Home-made plum butter and its friends–La Siesta chili con queso sauce (Topeka, Kansas) and O'Connor's mustard (Grand Forks, North Dakota).

Our shortcut to a plum butter and chile barbeque sauce
is to mix plum butter with Mama Lupe's chili con queso
sauce. As I understand the story, this is the sauce developed
at the La Siesta cafe in the Oakland district of Topeka,
Kansas. Mixed with sharp cheddar, it made the chile con
queso for La Siesta, Home of the Chili con Queso, as they
like to say. Then the recipe was franchised out to a company
in Moundridge, Kansas, which bottles Mama Lupe's sauce.
Unfortunately Mama Lupe's is not distributed on the northern plains, but we can hope.

Until a couple of years ago the most garlic I had seen
grown in one place was in the late Carmen Alonzo's back
yard in Emporia, Kansas. Don Carmen, a composer of
corridos (traditional Mexican ballads) and repository of
dichos (proverbs), liked his garlic.

This makes the point that I had considered garlic more
as an ethnic tradition than as a commercial proposition.
Speaking in terms either of latitude or of culture, it seems
unlikely that garlic would flourish on the northern plains,
but as you read this, if you're curled up by a winter fire, a
substantial crop of scenty bulbs is lying dormant under the
snow, awaiting spring growth and summer harvest.

Some 32,000 row-feet belong to Clara Sue and Gary
Price, at Dakota Gardens and Herbs, just north of Minot,
North Dakota. They are pioneers of the contemporary
garlic frontier.

Clara Sue grew up on the family farm, worked as a
stock broker, and now serves in the state house of representatives. (She holds the seat formerly held by Brynhild
Haugland, the longest-continuous-service legislator in
American history–52 years in the North Dakota house.)

Gary, a California native, came to Minot during military service, married Clara Sue, and started a custom cabinet construction business, Cal-Dak Cabinets. On a small part of the family farm, they also began a market garden, raising vegetables and herbs for local sale.

In the spring of 1992 they put in a modest crop of elephant garlic (a leek, not a true garlic). It did poorly; Gary says they did "virtually everything" wrong. So they headed for California to study methods used by established garlic farmers. They decided thereafter to try true garlic varieties. The California growers kept saying it had to be grown as a winter crop, but the North Dakotans, considering their winters, remained skeptical. They started some in peat pots and planted some in the spring, harvesting a small crop. The weeds got away from them.

Bulbs planted in the fall of 1993 and spring of 1994 produced a good crop marketed, in braids and in bulk, through the Minot Farmer's Market in 1994. In addition Clara Sue began production of garlic vinegars and pickled cloves. The following fall they planted eleven varieties (both hard-neck and soft-neck), resulting in a 1995 harvest of more than 500 pounds. The vinegars and pickles are now selling in stores of the region.

It's been a matter of trial and error. If you decide to raise garlic in the middle of North Dakota, you don't have a history of research and development to rely on! There are others across the region interested in the same enterprise, though. In 1994 the growers got together and formed a marketing cooperative, the Great Northern Garlic Growers Co-op. They got some state grant money for marketing feasibility studies.

This is real grassroots development. Clara Sue and Gary put out the *Garlic Lovers Newsletter* to report their horticultural progress and to encourage culinary adventurism by the consuming public. I think Gary, who's handy in a shop, enjoys the technical challenges–devising planters and harvesters and peelers.

The most difficult aspect to the cultural methods of the crop is winter mulching. It would be good to lay down straw, but for a commercial-size operation, that gets unwieldy. If snow cover could be ensured and maintained, that would serve the purpose, but winds too often blow parts of the field clear. That leads to experiments with snow management, using fence, ridges, and crop strips to trap snow.

Research and extension people now take an interest in the garlic proposition. I wonder if there aren't a few Carmen Alonzos out there who could lend some expertise.

Rummaging around the greenhouses at Neil Holland's Sheyenne Gardens, Harwood, North Dakota, I found a tray of seedling groundcherries. I never heard of anyone raising these in a garden, so I asked Neil about them. Sure, he said, lots of women in these parts used to raise groundcherries in their gardens, although not many do anymore. Plant some this year, he said, and you'll never have to do it again, because they reseed themselves.

I took some home and planted them at the West Fargo Branch Station for Applied Alternative Horticulture, meaning my back yard, and so this is a good place to note that NOT ONE FEDERAL DOLLAR WAS EXPENDED FOR EXPERIMENTS LEADING TO THIS ESSAY! For this important work I got not so much as a lowly graduate assistant to hoe out the pigweeds.

Anyway, while the groundcherries grew, I read up on
them in Kay Young's book, *Wild Seasons* (University of
Nebraska Press). Groundcherries, a nightshade plant, were
indeed used from the wild by women up and down the
plains and also seeded into their gardens for handy picking.
According to the *Flora of the Great Plains*, various species
of groundcherries are native to all parts of the plains from
Texas to North Dakota.

The yellow fruits grow inside paper-like husks, in the
manner of ornamental Chinese lanterns or Mexican tomatillos. When ripe, they drop from the branches, after which
you pick them up and strip off the husks.

Groundcherries, like rhubarb, served earlier generations
of plains folk as a fruit substitute. Kay gives recipes for
groundcherry marmalade, groundcherry pie, groundcherry
jam, and so on.

Being awash in fruits and berries around our house, I
thought about fitting these old fruits into a new culinary
niche. Good Mexican cookbooks, I knew, go on and on
about the virtues of tomatillos for making salsa. Groundcherries being close kin and physically similar to tomatillos, I
made the logical leap. Tasting a couple, and finding them
sweet and rich in flavor, I decided they would be good in
salsa, especially combined with the other fresh stuff coming
from our garden.

It worked, and I don't need any consumer focus group
to tell me this is great salsa. Simple, too. Just get out your
food processor and chop up, say, three parts groundcherries,
two parts green chiles, and one part onion. Throw in a
couple of cloves of garlic (which we've been growing since
learning about it from Clara Sue and Gary) and some
cilantro (what some people call Mexican parsley or Chinese

parsley or coriander) leaves. Maybe a little salt. Heat a little olive oil in a pan, add the chopped groundcherries and so on, heat the mix to boiling, and remove it from the heat– you just want to get the flavors to mingle.

Wonderful flavors. This salsa has heat, it has sweet, and the flavors are deep, not acidic.

Alumni and friends of a certain land-grant university on the northern plains will note that this salsa is, as the originator has named it, "The Yellow and the Green."

One problem is that on the plains there are people who raise groundcherries in their gardens, and people who raise chiles in their gardens, but not many who raise groundcherries and chiles in their gardens. Those are two different sets of people. Perhaps they should get together.

I better start watching where I put my feet. I think I just stepped right into a metaphor.

No good reason, I usually say. Because if the person has to ask, then it's going to be too much trouble to explain, I figure. The question is something like, Why are you making sauerkraut? Or oatmeal sausage, or horseradish, or apple butter, to stay with autumn things.

Maybe if I address the question seriously once, and answer honestly, that will settle it. So here goes. Three answers.

The first is one touched on in a book I reviewed–David Carpenter's book about living on the prairies, *Courting Saskatchewan*. The idea here is seasonal ritual. I like having a calendar that is marked up with things that depend on thawing and frost. With sauerkraut, for instance, the calendar begins in April, starting the cabbage seedlings, and continues in May with setting them out. They don't take a lot of care through the summer, but come September it's time to harvest and cut kraut, followed by a month or so of aroma-sniffing and scum-skimming before it's finished–in time to stuff some mallards with kraut and apples.

The second reason is simple taste. I'm not one of those Great Plains writers who portrays regional life as some sort of monastic asceticism or sensory deprivation. My favorite author is Wallace Stegner, who titled his Great Plains memoir *Wolf Willow*–the only book I know to be named for a smell. Life around here is full of the stuff of the senses, such as the smell of the kraut seeping up from the basement as I write. When you cry into your own horseradish as you grind it, or bite into an apple butter-and-oatmeal sausage sandwich, life is good.

Wallace Stegner boyhood home, Eastend, Saskatchewan. Wolf willow grows on the river bank in back.

These are two pretty straightforward reasons, but before I get to my third one, I want to make sure I'm not misunderstood. I am not one of these new sensitive guys. I'm a grouse hunter and even enjoy a cigar on occasion.

But there are all these things that women used to be responsible for, and that need to be taken care of, and they're just not. Most women my age think it's lame to do domestic things. They say my Grandma Meta and Aunt Emma were victims and drudges. (It's easy for them to say that, lacking personal acquaintance with those ladies.)

Women my age liberated themselves from all that. Their daughters, such as my university students, haven't a clue.

We can't put people back in their boxes. The old gender roles of farm life–roles created by women as much as by men, because they helped to keep life comprehensible–are not going to be restored. Few of this millennial generation ever knew those ways, and anyway, the people who say those rigid roles limited individual options are right.

The problem is that now people don't know the seasons, they don't know the senses, and they don't know their grandmothers. When we disparage what our grandmothers did and make them out to have been victims of domesticity, we say that their lives were meaningless. Well, they weren't. These women did worthwhile things of which we now suffer the loss.

So I want to honor them by doing what they did. If it shatters your stereotypes to find out a guy who prefers to drive a pickup can make apple butter, that's your problem. (I remember the time I brought a feminist university woman friend a house gift of chokecherry syrup, and she instructed me to thank my wife for it.)

Seventy years ago Alba Bales, the founding dean of home economics at North Dakota Agricultural College, introduced a startling new college course designed to educate young men about family issues and domestic science. We still have those sorts of courses. What we don't teach these guys, though, and what they need to know in order to honor women through the generations, is how to make apple butter.

17. Pasture People

The great virtue of the American West, both to those who study it and to those who live in it, is its space. It is not exactly rural. Most people in the West, including plains folk, live in towns and cities, and even those living in the country spend much of their time in town or going to and fro. But in between there is space.

To some, this means horizons unbroken by human works. Or the calls of cicadas and coyotes at dusk. Or the scent of sage as it brushes your trousers, or even of soil.

Space means something else, too, about human relations. It means that because people cross paths less frequently, the intersections are clearer and more memorable. You are not lost in the crowd. In a region as broad as the North American plains, individuals and families can be long distances apart and yet be connected in important ways.

I have spent quite a bit of time researching the history of the Rogler Ranch, of Chase County, Kansas. This ranch got its start in 1859 when Charles W. Rogler took up a pre-emption claim along the South Fork of the Cottonwood River. His bottomland farm, as did many in the surrounding Flint Hills, evolved into more of a ranch than a farm, as his son, Henry, became a prominent pasture man.

The business of a pasture man was to connect absentee landowners (living in places like Kansas City) with absentee cattle owners (living and keeping cowherds in places like West Texas). The cattle owners shipped their steers into the hills for the grazing season, at the conclusion of which they marketed them as grass-fattened beef. The pastureman took care of the cattle on pasture and saw them shipped out.

Tastes and methods in beef have changed somewhat, but Charles Rogler's grandson, Wayne, remained a big-time pastureman. People such as his father and he were individual links across a great agricultural region. That's one reason that the Rogler Ranch is not only of local interest but also historically significant enough to be placed on the National Register of Historic Places.

Another reason, in this era of environmental consciousness, is that the Roglers for generations have been taking care of grass. When Wayne, in crusty fashion, or his wife Elizabeth, much more poetically, extolls the virtues of native bluestem, they speak from long and practical experience, but even urban folk with no such experience respond sympathetically.

Now, since I started out talking about people connecting across great open spaces, let me introduce another member of the Rogler family—Wayne's brother, George. Lotte and I had the pleasure of meeting him in Mandan, North Dakota.

What do you suppose is his life's work up there? Taking care of grass. George Rogler is probably the country's foremost authority on crested wheat grass.

In the eyes of most Dakotans, Mandan, North Dakota, is to Bismarck what Fort Pierre, South Dakota, is to Pierre: the rowdy neighbor-town west across the Missouri where the bars stay open late.

Mandan also is the home, however, of the Northern Great Plains Research Center. It was there we found

George Rogler—as his family has done through the years
down in Kansas—taking care of grass. More specifically, we
came to talk to him about crested wheat grass.

Crested wheat grass is not well known to southern
plains folk, but it is a wondrous boon to stockmen of the
northern plains, both American and Canadian. A Siberian
species (or complex of species), it was introduced to the
United States in 1898 by Niels E. Hansen, the plant ex-
plorer.

Hansen, a plant breeder affiliated with the South
Dakota Agricultural Experiment Station, was a flamboyant
wheeler and dealer who made a lot of enemies in the
agricultural research establishment. Consequently, his
early introductions of crested wheat grass were sent out
and lost. He arranged for additional seed a few years later,
and some of this survived in experiment station plots.

Largely through the efforts of scientist A.C. Dillman,
seed and plantings were perpetuated at the Belle Fourche
(South Dakota) Experiment Station and at Mandan. That
was where George Rogler entered the story.

From the family ranch in Chase County, Kansas, Rogler
had gone to Kansas State for a degree in agronomy, received
in 1935. He worked briefly for the Soil Conservation
Service in Kansas, married Vera, and moved to a new
position at Mandan in 1936.

At that very time, crested wheat grass was being belat-
edly discovered by farmers, ranchers, and scientists of the
northern plains. As dust storms whipped wheat land into
dunes and blowouts, they sought to restore grass to stabilize
the soil. Often this took place in American national grasslands or in Canadian community pastures, where the

government stepped in to retire acres from cultivation and establish grass.

The problem was that as the drought and winds continued, they couldn't get a stand of native grass. Other than Russian thistle, which mercifully moved into the blown-out lands with the wind, little vegetation could stand the conditions—except for crested wheat grass.

Crested wheat grass became, in the words of one agricultural writer, "the best healer of these man-made wounds" of wind erosion. Despite being planted with cobbled-up equipment on poorly prepared ground, crested wheat grass grew.

People familiar with the situation on the southern plains at the same time will recall that it was nigh impossible to get grass established on blown-out ground until the drought ended. Unfortunately, they had no such introduced grass so well adapted to the southern plains as crested wheat grass was to the north.

Over the next couple of decades something else about the grass became plain. Crested wheat grass came on earlier in the spring than native grass. It also became unpalatable during summer. This meant that it could be grazed hard early, thus deferring use of the native grass. This sort of complementary grazing gives crested wheat grass a permanent place in range management.

Meanwhile, back at Mandan, Rogler, even now in his retirement, takes care of grass. We went out to have a look at the 1915 plots, the oldest known surviving planting of crested wheat grass in North America. Rogler was dismayed at the weeds in the neglected plots.

George Rogler inspects North America's oldest stand of crested wheat grass, Mandan, North Dakota.

Here on the American plains, we don't have anything quite like the community pastures they have in the prairie provinces of Canada. They are similar in origin to our national grasslands, but they operate differently. When you visit some community pastures, you realize that the Canadians have some good ideas how to live on the plains.

Community pastures, like national grasslands, began as a result of the great blow-outs of the 1930s. The government of Canada decided that much of the land that was blowing away should be bought back from farmers, seeded to grass, and used as pasture. This work was done by an agency called the Prairie Farm Rehabilitation Administration–sort of like the Soil Conservation Service and the Extension Service rolled into one.

Seeding crews came in to plant crested wheat grass, fencing crews constructed perfect fence lines straight as arrows, and the PFRA community pastures were ready for stocking. The plan was that these pastures were to benefit small to mid-sized farmer-stockmen putting in a few head each. This would encourage mixed farming in the area.

Keith Young, lanky and denim-clad, is the manager of the Wellington Community Pasture, in southern

Saskatchewan. His wife, Janet, has a job in town. We talked for a while in the yard, while the kids, Candy and Blade, fooled around down at the barn with a litter of border collie pups. Then we took a pickup tour of the 10,000-hectare pasture. Blade got the gates.

Keith was a city boy from Regina who headed west for Maple Creek–in Saskatchewan's southwestern cattle country–to become a cowboy. He worked on a ranch there, then as a rider on a couple of PFRA pastures, before landing the job as manager at Wellington. He likes his work.

Springtime means riding a hundred miles of fence in preparation for filling the pasture. Most of this and other work is horseback, although he has to trailer his horse to far parts of the pasture.

Come May, the sixty-some pasture patrons bring their cows and calves in. They choose which field they want their cows in–a Hereford field, a Charolais field, or a Simmental field. The PFRA supplies all three flavors of bulls, each bull branded with a DC (Dominion of Canada) on the right hip and a 22 (Wellington Community Pasture) on the right shoulder.

The cattle are cared for by the manager and his riders through the grazing season. They water in dugouts–trenches scraped out to hold snow melt, some refreshed by windmills.

The cattle have to be removed by 31 October. On designated days the riders, some temporary riders (including a couple of cowgirls), and the patrons get together and gather the cattle from each field, loading them out through an excellent set of PFRA pens.

Keith feeds the bulls through the winter at the headquarters. By spring they get pretty restive and tend to smash up the pens.

As we toured the pasture, sharptail grouse burst from the grass—good grass this year, recovered from the previous year's drought. In a slough developed by Ducks Unlimited, little teal were paddling around. On a hot day, the cattle were mostly hanging around the dugouts.

As I said, Keith likes his job, mostly because of the style of life it offers. As he sees it, a PFRA community pasture is cowboy heaven.

"It's a different way of living on the prairie," he says. "You can't beat it, if you ask me."

Border collie pups are one of the benefits of community pasture life for Keith Young and his family.

People used to say, "It's a small world," when they came across something or someone familiar in a faraway place. Nowadays, when they want to say something just as dumb, but sound more sophisticated, they say something like, "It's a global village."

So I'm not going to say either of those things, but I am going to say that despite the great length and breadth of the Great Plains, there are some things you keep coming across. Like the Matador Land and Cattle Company.

The Matador was a Scottish syndicate set up to establish a 1.5 million-acre cattle ranch in West Texas. Its holdings subsequently sprawled across a half-dozen states, its headquarters moved to Colorado, and the organization survived to mid-twentieth century. Early in this century, the Matador's northward quest for new range led it into western Canada.

W.M. Pearce, Vice President of Texas Tech University, wrote a fine history of the Matador, published in 1964. He recounts how in 1903 Murdo Mackenzie of the Matador came up to Swift Current, Assiniboia (later Saskatchewan), and looked over some range on the Saskatchewan River. "The grass is better than anything I have ever seen," he reported, "and there is an abundance of water." Consequently, in 1905 the Matador shipped a herd from Alamositas, Texas, to its new 50,000-acre Canadian Division, land leased from the Canadian government.

I first heard of the far-flung Matador operations from Elmer Cooper, an old-time Flint Hills cowboy about whom Jim has written eloquently. Elmer recalled how the Matador used to ship aged steers three and four years old from Texas and Colorado to stock pastures in the Flint Hills. These steers had hardly ever seen a man before, and they were the wildest beasts Elmer can ever recall handling.

On a tour of western Canada I ran across remnants of the Matador again. It turns out that during the post-war break of the beef market in 1921, the Matador liquidated the Canadian Division. Its lease went back to the government, but economic conditions were so bad that no other outfit wanted it. So the province of Saskatchewan took over and operated it as a community pasture, where small livestock operators could each put a few head (up to a couple hundred) for the grazing season.

I found the records about this in the Saskatchewan Archives, Regina. But I also got out to have a look at the old Matador range itself, which is still operated as a provincial community pasture. What was the valley of the Saskatchewan River is now Lake Diefenbaker, which the Matador pasture overlooks from the north. It is, as Mackenzie noted, splendid and well-watered range, with enough rugged canyons for wintering of stock.

In the nearby town of Kyle I found John Remple, who worked at the pasture from 1943 on and was its manager from 1963 to 1984. No one knows the old Matador range like John Remple does. His wife, Mary, also can tell you a lot about living there.

There is something to be said for taking root like prairie grass in some particular part of the plains, learning to know it intimately, having a sense of place. John Remple worked at the Matador from 1943 to 1984–starting as a seasonal hand, moving his young family into a shack at what they called the East Camp, becoming foreman in 1950, promoted to manager in 1963. Mary shared that life, and they both relished it.

The tape rolls, and grown kids keep running in and out, as for two hours the Rempels recount their experiences over a kitchen table, then get out the photograph albums. With the coffee, out pours an account full of data for analysis later–historical accounts of co-operative farms at the pasture, good information on range management, details about pasture operations.

But even before you have time to go over your tapes and notes, you know that you have learned something, or at least been reminded of something, more important than the details. I'm talking about the possibility of living a full life, one full of hard work but not the worse for it, in the middle of a challenging, spectacular landscape. That's what the Rempels did at the Matador.

Mary keeps laughing about starting out in a two-room shanty, cooking on a wood stove for six or eight or more hands, plus pasture patrons bringing in their stock for the grazing season, plus branding crews, fencing crews, and you never knew who else. About raising their own garden, chickens, hogs, and beeves. About moving again and again, and getting the kids to distant schools. Someone needs to go up there to Kyle and tell her how exploited she was.

And John, too—riding some 200 miles of fence in the spring, dipping split cedar posts, setting them in all types of rocky soil, fixing the gaps across all those coulees, stringing up the wire brought down by snow banks. Bringing the cattle in by ford and ferry across the Saskatchewan River. Heeling and wrestling all the calves. Rounding up and loading out twelve, sixteen carloads at a time for Winnipeg, every two weeks from July to September. Putting up enough prairie wool hay to feed (with a team) 200 government bulls (each one branded with the outline of a wheat sheaf, for the province of Saskatchewan) through the winter. And after becoming manager, finishing up a day's work on the range, then staying up sometimes until 3:00 a.m. to get the books right and the paperwork straight with the province.

I know that the province never paid its pasture people liberally. What benefits could balance off such labor?

I can't answer that question. I don't know how to calculate the value of good company, of the cast of characters—hands and pasture patrons—that continually trooped through the headquarters. I know it must be worth something, too, to have your family working with you, and for horse people to have a situation wherein working with horses shades into playing with horses. For a lot of us it would be worth quite a bit to be able to leave horseback from your own yard for an antelope hunt.

I'm still not sure how it all adds up. Maybe if I listen to the tapes again, and study the albums some more, I'll figure it out.

18. Lost Forest

Years ago my wife and I gave up taking vacations, because we found that no matter how attractive the scenery, we couldn't get along with time on our hands. We travel now more than ever, of course, but it's always with some purpose besides a holiday.

We like it that way. We travel in the style of the authors of great travel narratives. John Steinbeck, for instance (in *Travels with Charley*), who felt he needed to re-discover the American character. Or Francis Parkman (in *The Oregon Trail*), who burned to see wild Indians at war. When you travel with a quest, you're in good company.

One quest took us into some of the finest, loneliest country we've explored. I have recounted some of our travels to community pastures in western Canada. In one of these, near Kindersley, Saskatchewan, we went looking for a lost forest–an artificial forest of Scotch pine, planted back in the 1930s in the middle of a vast expanse of grassland.

Armed with a good Saskatchewan grid map, we made our way from Kindersley out to the community pasture. We stopped once to chase a red fox out of a culvert and watch him run. At the pasture, we found the manager gone, but his son, Steve Hoffman, agreed to be our guide.

He was a good one. He loaded us into a PFRA government pickup and set out across the township-sized pasture, getting the gates himself. He pointed out the dugouts, the new electric cross-fences, and the remains of a schoolhouse, including the old school well, which the cattle use for a rub. He talked about living there, and about the Hutterite colony just to the north.

And he took us to the forest, a forty-acre enclave fenced off from the cattle. This was an odd experiment, which I knew about from reading the original records over at the Indian Head tree farm. The municipal fathers of Kindersley had proposed during the dead days of the depression to begin this tree plantation, and the government had given them the trees.

A PFRA pasture manager's pickup delivered us to where prairie meets the Kindersley forest.

The trees, planted by a local crew, never had much care. They just listed a north-facing sandy hillside and planted the seedlings in the furrows—no water, no cultivation, just a web-wire fence to keep out jackrabbits in those droughty, rabbit-plagued days.

Unbelievably, the Scotch pines thrived. When you approach the site today, the plantation appears as a dark blotch on the pale hillside-horizon. You park, and the effect is surreal as you step suddenly from prairie into forest. We wondered what made us feel so strange, and then realized that it was a sound. Even more than the evergreen foliage and dense shade, the hissing rustle of the wind among the boughs seemed out of place.

Deer fawn here. Great horned owls, Swainson's and ferruginous hawks, and golden eagles frequent the place and nest here—we saw a golden eagle sitting on the prairie a hundred yards away.

In 1982, when Steve's dad had just taken over as pasture manager, he got a call from some municipal officials who said they were on their way out to dig up the pines and transplant them to a golf course. Hoffman hopped in the pickup with a gun, drove out, and told the workmen, "You take any of those trees and you're done for."

Good for him. He keeps the fence up, too.

When you go fishing, sometimes you catch something you aren't fishing for, and that's just luck.

My Lotte and I spent most of one summer traveling across the Canadian prairies studying shelterbelts. Coming from the southern plains, we recall the Shelterbelt Project of the 1930s and figure we know quite a bit about the subject. Our organized shelterbelt plantings have been different from the Canadian, however. Ours are multi-row plantings, with rows of several species planted alongside one another to form a broad belt. (Similar, in fact, to the way they planted them in the Soviet Union.) Canadian shelterbelts are single-row affairs. They plant one of several species—poplar, Siberian elm, green ash—but most of all, a Russian leguminous shrub called caragana.

So one weekend we were in Indian Head, Saskatchewan; we'd been going through documents at the government tree farm there. We decided on a Sunday to run up and see some local tree-planters, John and Christine Rumancik.

The name is Czech. John's immigrant grandparents settled here—just north of the splendid Qu'Appelle Valley—and started planting trees around the place immediately. Christine's ancestry is German and Australian.

As we drove up on the grid road, the old home place was on our left, to the south. That's where John's parents, Gilbert and Magda, live. The stands of evergreens enveloping the farmstead are magnificent—blue spruce, Colorado spruce. Within their shelter, Magda raises a beautiful flower garden, including an impressive stand of poppies, raised not only for their color but also for the seed, used in baking.

We spent a couple of hours going around the farm in John's pickup, looking over his demonstration shelterbelts. Each one is a different species being observed for its hardiness and its economic benefits. John likes the green ash best. The Siberian elm die out early, and the poplar send suckers out in the wheat.

Going back to John and Christine's house, across the road north from the old home place, we saw that they were keeping up the homestead tree-planting tradition of the family. Plantings in various stages of growth were all around.

Lotte was most impressed, though, by Christine's garden. It was flourishing with peas, potatoes, squash, lettuce, other vegetables, and most of all, enormous cabbages. She not only makes her own sauerkraut, but also freezes whole cabbages so that she can make galuskies (big cabbage rolls) any time of the year.

Leaving the yard again, we rode with John out to a couple of bluffs (a bluff here is a stand of native trees, not a cliff) to check out some of the native fruits—saskatoons (juneberries to folks south of 49°) and chokecherries. Later that day, he and Christine were going out to pick saskatoons

John Rumancik, tree planter, wades into a bluff in search of saskatoons, near Fort Qu'Appelle, Saskatchewan.

for pies. They were ripe—juicy maroon.

Anyway, we learned a lot about shelterbelts, but we came away with something else, too. We were thinking, How many times, when you drive into a plains farm-yard today, do you get the impression that the residents are living there because they really want to live right there? In how many places does it seem that people are putting in roots—literally, in the case of tree-planters—and envisioning a future? And do you acquire the sort of attachment and vision that the Rumanciks have by the exercise of putting in roots, or do you have to have it in the first place in order to make the effort?

Conquest. Great name for a town. A name filled with the optimism, determination, and romance of the settlement era. But by 1935 Conquest, Saskatchewan, seemed just one more town about to be snuffed out by dust and depression.

I was far away, in a genteel place, when I learned of the crisis in Conquest. Seated at a polished oak table in the reading room of the Public Archives of Canada, Ottawa, I had a commanding view north, through floor-to-ceiling windows, of the broad and shimmering Ottawa River.

My call slip brought me a box of letters from Record Group 17, Records of the Ministry of Agriculture, and there was Conquest, 2000 miles away, as described by F.H. Jones, Chairman of the Conquest Field Shelterbelt Association, 4 April 1935.

The crisis of those times had brought forth, in certain fortunate communities of the plains, leaders such as Jones and his friend, Peter Kennedy. They were tree-planters. They had organized their neighbors into the shelterbelt association and proposed massive shelterbelt plantings in their locality, with the assistance of provincial officials and nurserymen. They had their trees. All they wanted from the federal government in 1935 was $250 to help get them in the ground, since they had to be planted at the same time the farmers seeded their spring wheat.

Somehow they must have raised the necessary cash, for over the next decade the people at Conquest planted well over three million shelterbelt trees. The first ones–a million, perhaps– were planted by hand. The planter opened a spade-hole, slipped a seedling in, stepped on it, stepped forward one step, and opened another hole, proceeding thus across the section and back.

Peter Kennedy got this started. He had planted his own shelterbelts early in the 1920s, and their example–especially the way they stopped wind erosion–convinced neighbors and governmental officials to go along with the project. Kennedy also became Secretary of the shelterbelt association.

So Lotte and I went out to Conquest to see this, see what was left of the community and its plantings. Driving into the locality was a peculiar experience. Turning off the highway onto grid roads approaching Conquest, we felt like we were like entering a garden, everything hedged and bounded. I had a hard time taking photographs that I thought would capture anything like the sense of the place.

Then over to nearby Outlook, in search of Hugh Kennedy, son of the founder of the shelterbelt association, retired to town. We went into his living room, began taping the interview, and something seemed strangely familiar. We got the story and some hospitality, too, but only later did I realize what seemed strange about the situation.

As we listened to Hugh Kennedy tell the Conquest story, our gazes swiveled to his picture windows, facing west toward Conquest. And below us lay a spectacular scene, the broad valley of the Saskatchewan River, pale pelicans cruising its bars. Once more I got the story of Conquest, and in a setting so congenial, so pleasing that Conquest again seemed 2000 miles away.

I do a lot of my work in fine chambers like the reading room of the Public Archives of Canada. And when I get back to investigations on the plains, the people there, like the Kennedys, are so hospitable that they insulate me from some of the hard facts of their history. But never let me forget those guys with spades in Conquest.

19. Parking for North Dakotans

Public art is risky. The state of Nebraska went to a lot of trouble and expense to place modern sculpture all along Interstate 80, but people don't much care for it. Instead, they flock around the big bronzes of battling elk outside the Cabela's store in Sidney. Fargo, North Dakota, brought in an acclaimed Chicano artist to place a ceramic sculpture at the corner of Broadway and Main, and people have been carping ever since. In Kansas, the state capitol murals by John Stueart Curry were the source of considerable controversy over the image of the state.

On the other hand, public art can instill community pride and provide individual comfort. I remember checking into a motel in Wamego, Kansas, not long after my first book, a history of custom wheat harvesting, was published. On the north outside motel wall, someone had painted a beautiful red No. 27 Massey combine. That made me feel at home, as I'm sure it did every custom cutter who stayed there.

It seemed like a straightforward and good idea when the Foster County, North Dakota, commissioners decided, as part of the county centennial in 1983, to have a series of murals painted for the halls of the beautiful old courthouse in Carrington. They commissioned four artists, each to depict an era in the county's history. The four were Helen Johnson, for the era 1883-1915; R.A. "Lefty" Wenstrom, for 1915-40; Rosemary Voglewede, for 1940-65; and Sandi Dahl, for 1965-83.

I got the story of the origin of the murals from long-time county commissioner John Murphy. He also took me on a dandy cook's tour of the courthouse, including a swing through the courtroom and a climb up onto the roof for a great view of the town and area.

I spent some time studying the four murals. The first three artists—Johnson, Wenstrom, and Voglewede—are local people not necessarily renowned as painters, but the documentary aspects of their works are interesting. They covered their big canvases with smaller images, little vignettes, each a story we are encouraged to consider part of the official recollection of community history.

The key image in the first mural, then, is a woman doing wash in front of a tarpaper shack. The railroad is arriving, the Kirkwood Hotel is built, homesteads are being taken—it's a country in the making.

In the second mural, progress and problems are mingled. There's a big threshing rig, a sulky plow, a buggy giving way to an auto. But a soldier is taking fond leave of his family, and facsimiles of grain and livestock receipts show the depressed prices of the 1930s. The community is being tested.

In the third mural, the community is triumphant. Soldiers go off and defeat the Axis and the Communists (sort of). New homes and machine sheds rise, along with a hospital, a radio station, a high school, and churches. People are engaging in commerce and also enjoying a new swimming pool, a golf course, and local lakes. This is a busy, busy painting.

I noticed something about the progression of paintings. There are sixteen people in the first, twenty-some in the second, and forty-one in the third. I understand that Mrs.

Voglewede had fourteen kids, who were growing up during the era she depicted, but I don't think her family situation accounts for the busy populace comprised in her perspective. I think her painting reflects what we in the Great Plains were thinking in the post-World War II generation. We were positive about the future. We saw a future here for our kids.

What a contrast, then, with the final painting. It is a landscape, the dominant figure in which is a Steiger tractor. The only human visible, dimly, is the driver, in the cab. The landscape is attractive, and it is productive—I see wheat, cattle, and sunflowers, combines at work, and a Harvestore blue jug. But I don't see people.

Sandi Dahl is a professional artist from Devil's Lake, now resident in Fargo. She was painting the historical era of her own generation. In preparation for her work, she says, she toured the countryside with John Murphy. She produced a painting that is sound in both aesthetic and documentary aspects. It's a true image. And that's why it's troubling.

If good art makes us think, then by that standard, the Foster County murals are good indeed.

In Tukwila, a southern suburb of Seattle, we found a corner grocery store—Bernie and Boys Inc.—with a sign that seemed to beckon directly to us. It was a Mr. Whipple-like life-size silhouette holding a placard that said, "Parking for North Dakotans Only. All Others Will Be Towed." This, about a thousand miles west of the western border of North Dakota.

The explanation lies in the western migration of plains folk. I'm from Kansas, and I have relatives in Oregon.

Everybody in Oklahoma has kin in California, where "Okie"
became a generic term referring to anyone who came there
via old Route 66. From North Dakota the common line of
migration moves straight along latitudinal lines to Washington state. It's usually assumed that the migration of people
from the plains to the west coast happened because of the
Depression and Dust Bowl. In fact, the growth of industry in
the west coast states during and after World War II was what
attracted most of them.

Boeing, in Seattle, for instance. And as Dakotans
aggregated in the area, grocer Bernardo Salle–who with his
father began his business in 1937–noticed. "Because 85
percent of the people that leave North Dakota come to
Seattle," he explains, "and that started in the early '40s
during World War II, when they came out here and
worked at Boeing and the shipyards."

This fellow has a strange sense of salesmanship. He bills
his store as "Home of the Live Butcher." I'm still not sure
what that means, but it sounds better than the alternative.

So these North Dakotans kept coming in, especially the
German-Russians, and asking for spices to make their own
country sausage. Salle caught on, started making sausage the
way they wanted it, and advertised "North Dakota Country
Style Sausage" for sale. "One thing led to another, and we
got in the North Dakota kick," he says. "Now everybody
thinks I'm from North Dakota. I was born right down the
road here a mile and a half."

Next Salle started selling Cloverdale meats from
Mandan and Dakota Kid sunflower seeds. He contacted
Leonardo's of Cando, but never succeeded in arranging a
pasta supply. (This is an Italian grocery, remember.) And
he got a printer to make up these "Parking for North Dako-

tans Only" signs, which sell briskly. (Since coming back
from Seattle, I've noticed several of them in driveways in
North Dakota towns.)

Several restaurants in Tukwila now serve North Dakota
Country Sausage. One recently debuted the Dakota Burger,
made with a sausage patty.

"If I had a tavern," Salle says, "I would have two of
them. These people from North Dakota, they are good
beer drinkers. I'd have one called North Dakota and the
other South Dakota, and it would work, I'm sure it would."

These Dakotans are good customers, too, Salle remarks:
"They are frugal people, a little on the tight side, but they
always pay for what they get." And loyal–young people
come in and buy stuff and say, "My dad was from North
Dakota."

I took a picture of Salle, "the Live Butcher," behind his
meat counter. One Salle son, Mike, was working in the
store; three others–Joe, Tom, and John–were over in a
second store.

This Dakota outpost got me to thinking. The Okie
migration is commonly credited for important cultural
developments in California–the Bakersfield sound in country music, the Reagan phenomenon in politics. I wonder
what impact the Dakotans have had on the Pacific Northwest?

People in North Dakota are accustomed to out-migration. Bernie Salle posts his "Parking for North Dakotans
Only" sign outside his store because of all the Dakotans who
have moved to the Seattle vicinity. I took a poll of my
freshman History class one day–some 180 students. About
two-thirds said they had relatives in Washington state;

Bernardo Salle, the Live Butcher of Tukwila, Washington, caters to expatriate North Dakotans.

about half had kin in Arizona. I forgot to ask about Minneapolis.

We usually say this exodus started in 1930, the census year when our population peaked. It has declined ever since, until the reversal of the current decade. In fact, I now learn, the out-migration started earlier than 1930, and you may be surprised where the departing Dakotans were going.

Canada. The frontier did not come to a close at Williston, or even at Shelby. It just moved on to Saskatchewan and Alberta.

Dr. R. Bruce Shepard, of the University of Saskatchewan, visited us in Fargo and told us the extent of the migration of Americans into the prairie provinces. He contends this "was likely the largest out-migration ever of people from the United States." For Canadians, it "was likely the largest migration into their country." The American migration to the Canadian prairies peaked during the years 1911-13.

This makes sense, when you think about it. Elwyn Robinson, in his classic history of North Dakota, writes of the hard times around 1911 and the large number of farmers leaving the state, especially from north-central areas, along the Soo Line. Well, the Soo Line runs right into southwestern Saskatchewan, where it links up with the Canadian Pacific. Mighty convenient.

Shepard has found record of 43,800 homestead entries by North Dakotans–more than from any other state–in western Canada during the years 1893-1921. He has a map of western Canada that shows an "American belt" of settlement filling the area between Regina, Saskatoon, Edmonton, and Calgary.

Among the North Dakotans heading north and west from North Dakota was a boy named Wallace Stegner, who, after growing up in Eastend, Saskatchewan, would become America's greatest Western writer. Also a part of the same exodus was Stephan G. Stephansson, the distinguished Icelandic poet, who ended up in a new Icelandic settlement in Alberta.

It appears there were wholesale relocations of North Dakota communities, including several aggregations of Germans from Russia (who, I suppose, thereby became Canadian Germans from Russia via America). Beiseker, Alberta, northeast of Calgary, is named for the banker from North Dakota who promoted its settlement.

The American migrants to Canada were visible and influential. Unlike many of the other settlers of the Canadian prairies, the Americans were experienced, mechanized farmers who brought carloads of equipment with them. They headed for the open plains. Other immigrants, such as the Ukrainians, might prefer the parklands with their bluffs and sloughs, but the Americans went to places where they could cut long, straight furrows. Their farms, on the average, were larger than those of their new neighbors.

We need a new billboard at Portal to welcome our
Canadian kin coming down to shop in Minot. It should say,
"Welcome to North Dakota–Birthplace of Prairie Canada."

Snow was drifted level with the county blacktop road,
so the shoulders were indistinguishable. Early dark had
fallen. The northwest wind whipped and curled blankets
through our beams, now and then billowing up to mask the
windshield with white darkness. A bad night for driving. A
good night for Class B basketball.

Part of the appeal of high-school basketball is the
contrast between harsh exterior, the winter night, and warm
interior, the school gym. Most small-high school gyms of
recent construction look a lot like machine sheds, but
packed with people and activity, they don't seem stark.
Drop your coat on the pile in the hall, get your hand
stamped, and you enter a community.

Some plains states, like my current residence, North
Dakota, still refer to small-school ball as "Class B." Others,
like my native Kansas, have divided competition into more
classes and desig-
nated them all some
kind of "A"–AA,
AAA, and so on–so
that no one has to
be something less
than "A." I like
"Class B," because
it's unpretentious.

Oakes High School players and coaches
chart strategy for the annual Cowbell Game
with Ellendale, one of the great Class B
rivalries in North Dakota.

On the night
described above, we

took in a Class B game in a town of maybe 600 population. It was a close game, well attended. The home team had a go-to center on whom they relied down the stretch. The visitors, a more balanced team, pressed well and prevailed in the end.

This town lies in the Sheyenne River valley, sandhill country, great for white-tail deer. Front and center of the home section at the game was quite a bunch of fellows engaged in some sort of group thing, all wearing hunter orange—coveralls, ski masks, hats. None of them seemed to have girl friends. But then, none of them was accidentally shot that night, either.

I've been at Class B games where at half-time, the booster club sold bingo cards, and they played a card between halves. They didn't do that in this case, but I noticed after the game, most of the crowd stayed in the gym. Sure enough, pretty soon people were going around selling bingo cards. The more common post-game routine is for local parents to serve coffee and cokes and bars ("bars" being generic for any sweet you bake in a pan and cut into squares) to visiting players, cheerleaders, teachers, and parents.

I suppose this Class B school doesn't have much of a physics lab, and probably no art program at all. The library, though, was open during the game.

These days, the drive home from a game is often long. School consolidation continues, but in much of plains country, consolidation is an indefinite proposition. Schools combine, distances increase, economies of scale evaporate, and you never reach a point of sustainable efficiency. It's hard to figure where this will end.

If the choice comes down to efficiency on the one hand, and Class-B basketball and bars after the game on the other hand, I think I know which way I'll vote.

The North Dakota Department of Public Instruction reports that school closings have slowed–only one or two dissolved in a year–but that as rural depopulation continues, we can expect closings to resume apace. Agricultural economists project that as commodity subsidies end, more farms will fail. In public lectures across the region, I have been referring to the generation since 1950, my own time on the plains, as the "Last Picture Show Generation."

Now let me tell you about a wedding I attended. The bride was the beautiful, blond-haired, eldest daughter of a German Lutheran farm family in the middle of a plains state. The groom was a ranch boy and stock car racer from the western part of the state. When I arrived at the stone Gothic church, the groomsmen, including some Bohemian boys in tuxes and Stetsons, were sitting in the back of a tall pickup finishing off a case of beer.

Entering the church, I saw the organist going upstairs to the choir loft carrying a song folio that said on the cover, *Reba's Greatest Hits*. The preacher was a galvanized Baptist from Oklahoma who talked out the side of his mouth, even when he prayed, like maybe the Lord was behind him somewhere. Standing up with the bride was one of the beautiful Castillo girls.

After the ceremony the festivities shifted over to the Catholic parish hall, because it was the only place that would accommodate the 400 celebrants at the reception and dance. Food for the reception was being served by the

two fellows who live in the old hotel on the corner of Main
and Broadway; besides selling antiques, one of them has an
interior decorating business, the other is the town florist,
and they do a little catering, too. (I first met these guys
through the pages of the weekly newspaper, when they were
pictured on the front page as new businessmen being welcomed to town by the mayor, a pillar of the Knights of
Columbus.)

This was not the last picture show. This was the first
dance of the ball.

Don't these people read the sociological literature?
Don't they listen to the national news? Don't they know
that as plains folk, they are a breed destined for extinction?

I keep thinking about that wedding, about the mix of
people there mingling and mating and making their own
lives. While pompous commentators propound their
prescriptions for regional retrenchments or revival, these
young people of the plains are living the good life. Not for
them the sad, nostalgic study of faded photos in dusty
albums of high schools consolidated out of existence. Not
for them the fussing over fallen barns and abandoned
farmsteads, or the futile longing for the innocence of a
mythic past.

Nor do they think they are missing something because
they are not bathed nightly by the bright lights of Minneapolis or Denver or Los Angeles. Those are places for
weekends.

They aren't interested in arguing the relative merits of
the old red and the new blue hymnals, any more than they
are interested in drawing lines according to skin tone.

They have become native to the country.

The projections may well be right. More doors will close, more homesteads be left to rot. But that is a footnote, and should not obscure to us the main story.

A country may sift through quite a few people before it finds the right ones. Then it keeps them. In the Great Plains of North America, that process has just started. The country has sorted out a few Native Americans and some northern Europeans. There are lots more, perhaps better suited to the country, to try.

20. You Must Be from North Dakota

It all started with a feature in the newspaper column, *Plains Folk*, that was distributed across the region by NDSU Extension on the last day of 1997. Here's what it said.

Most Americans by now are familiar with Jeff Foxworthy's satires on Southern culture. In a self-effacing style similar to telling Norwegian jokes, he goes on forever with his catalog of good-old-boy qualities, all in the "If you (fill in the blank), then you might be a Redneck" format.

Now, what if we were to catalog the distinctive traits of North Dakotans in the same way? I already had been thinking about this for a while when I received a folklorish electronic communication from sources unknown headed, "You might be a North Dakotan if . . ."

"If you define summer as three months of bad sledding," this document intones, "you might be a North Dakotan." Or,

- If your definition of a small town is one that doesn't have a bar . . .
- If you can identify a Minnesota accent . . .
- If "down south" to you means Aberdeen . . .
- If you have no problem spelling "Wahpeton" . . .
- If you have an ICBM in your back yard . . .
- If you have as many Canadian coins in your pockets as American ones . . .
- If your kids' baseball and softball games have ever been snowed out . . .

- If you drive 70 mph on the highway and pass on the right . . .
- If at least 50% of your relatives smell like beets . . .
- If you don't understand what the big deal about Moorhead is . . .
- If people borrow things to you . . .

All right, I'm sure now you have the idea. I encourage you to read these out loud, with appropriate inflection, to get the full flavor.

What's more, I'm volunteering right now to be the official curator and cataloger of the "You might be a North Dakotan" register. I'll even contribute a few of my own to prime the pump:

- If you have ever served glorified rice at a wedding reception . . .
- If you refer to the state just east of you as "The People's Republic of Minnesota" . . .
- If you expect to be excused from school for deer season . . .
- If the *soup du jour* at your home-town cafe is always beer cheese or knoephla . . .
- If you like to send liberal Democrats to Congress and rock-ribbed Republicans to the statehouse . . .
- If your favorite hors'douvre is little weenies and barbeque sauce in a crockpot . . .
- If you refer to the blessed union of an ELCA Lutheran and a Missouri-Synod Lutheran as a "mixed marriage" . . .
- If you'd like to laugh at this, but you're afraid someone will notice you . . .

Then, I'd say, you might be from North Dakota. And you'd be capable of helping me out with this list. Offer limited to

North Dakota residents and expatriates (which means about half the people in Arizona and Washington state) and good people who **wish** they lived in North Dakota.

The response from the reading public to my appeal for North Dakota-isms was more than I expected, such that, despite my usual determination to respond personally to all communications by readers, I was compelled to resort to form letter.

The respondents numbered 86–53 from North Dakota, 6 from Minnesota, 3 from Massachusetts, 2 each from California, Iowa, South Dakota, Oregon, Idaho, Arizona, Wisconsin, Florida, and Kentucky, and 1 each from Montana, Colorado, Indiana, Virginia, and Maryland (plus one with no state attribution). I believe that all the responses from out of state were from expatriate North Dakotans or spouses of same.

I felt some trepidation as I began opening the wad of mail in my box. You see, when I arrived in North Dakota in 1992, it seemed to me that a spirit of backbiting defensiveness was abroad in the land. The anti-government, anti-everything attitude that was plaguing all of America at the time had exacerbated the traditional survivalism of the northern plains. Public officials were under siege and sometimes under fire, and I mean that literally. People were ready to fight about any little thing, or if there wasn't anything to fight about, they conjured something, like United Nations tanks massing in Manitoba, or conspiracies of homosexuals taking over public institutions.

I had poked fun at North Dakota. To me, of course, that is a sign of affection. I sometimes tell people in North Dakota about the preacher in my home church in western

Kansas—an Oklahoma Baptist converted to Lutheranism
who can't preach worth a fig, but everybody likes him. He
gets up in the pulpit and insults people, making disparaging
remarks about some woman's cooking, about some fellow's
bird dog, about the college some kid is attending. That's
how these people know he loves them. When I describe this
to North Dakota Lutherans, they don't get it. I had poked
fun at North Dakota, and I expected to be chastised.

So how many hostile letters did I get? None.

I'm convinced that between 1992 and 1997 something
important happened on the northern plains. I know that in
1992, for the first time since 1930, the population of North
Dakota increased. Economic renewal, too, ran way ahead of
the demographic resurgence. Most important, the public
mood of the region turned around. Confidence, or at least
hope, swelled. Cranks were no longer considered prophets,
but just cranks. And people enjoyed a good joke on themselves.

Now, as befits the spirit of the Dakota Circle, I'm going
to let the people of the Flickertail State have the last word.
Here are selected sayings from my catalog. Are you from
North Dakota?

- If you watch the weather channel and like it . . .
- If you drive to town during a blizzard just to see if the
  weather man knows what he's talking about . . .
- If you've ever said, "But it's a dry cold" . . .
- If you've spent the last 15 minutes getting your child
  dressed to play in the snow only to have him tell you
  he has to go potty now . . .
- If you design your Halloween costumes to fit over
  snowmobile suits . . .

- If you've attended a formal affair, in your best dress, wearing your finest jewelry and your Sorels . . .
- If somewhere in the state is a piece of frozen metal with bits of your tongue stuck to it . . .
- If your Easter bonnet had ear flaps . . .
- If your snowblower gets more affection than your wife . . .
- If the forecast is for 60 mph winds, 3 feet of snow, 60 below wind chills, and the highway is full of people from any small town going to any big city, even if it's 120 miles, just to shop, or for the absolutely necessary reason of attending a basketball tournament . . .

- If you think snow is supposed to fall horizontally . . .
- If there is no question of having a white Christmas; the question is whether you'll have a white Halloween or Easter or even Memorial Day . . .
- If you name blizzards . . . .
- If you lie awake thinking of uses for leafy spurge . . .
- If you remember one of your family

North Dakotan in winter plumage.

traditions as honking at the tree between New Rockford
and Carrington every time you passed it, because it was
the only tree around . . .

- If you cried when the tree was cut down . . .
- If, even after being gone for over 30 years, you still get
breathless looking at a field of sunflowers . . .
- If you get claustrophobic in other states where you can't
see the scenery for all the trees and mountains . . .
- If you assume everybody has seen northern lights and
sun-dogs, no big deal . . .
- If your ears pop going over the railroad bridge between
Fargo and Grand Forks . . .
- If you claim to be able to stand on a beer can and see
the whole state . . .
- If you know Ole and Lena personally . . .
- If improper grammar used by TV characters irritates you . . .
- If you think "initiative" means something to sign . . .
- If even though you're not breaking the law, you break
into a cold sweat when the game warden appears . . .
- If you think the opening of deer season is a national
holiday . . .
- If you honk the horn every time you go over the Red
River from Minnesota to North Dakota (while your kids
are hiding in the back seat from embarrassment) . . .
- If every time you see a Michelle Pfeiffer movie, you tell
everyone within earshot that her parents came from
New Rockford, and her Grandma still lives there . . .
- If you apply for a job as a nanny in Connecticut and the
only reference you need is your driver's license . . .
- If you still vote for William Langer as a write-in . . .
- If your children can read and write and do math and
stuff . . .

- If the current movie you want to go see in the local theatre has already become a "Classic" in the rest of the nation . . .
- If you can name one of the other entertainers on the Lawrence Welk Show . . .
- If you seal a deal with a handshake . . .
- If you never use your turn signal . . .
- If the area inside your front door is constantly piled with boots, shoes, etc. . . . . .
- If in high school you were a starter in three or more major sports since your freshman year . . .
- If you have a legitimate need for SUVs and know they have been around longer than this yuppie trend to own one . . .
- If you own only three spices–salt, pepper, and ketchup . . .
- If you only eat at restaurants with a salad bar . . .
- If you know where juneberries grow, what they are, and what to do with them . . .
- If at least three times a year your kitchen doubles as a meat processing plant . . .
- If you're asked by your transplanted aunts and uncles to bring a bottle of Everclear when you visit them in Washington and Oregon . . .
- If you think chokecherry jelly is the greatest jelly on earth . . .
- If your caterer and social director is the American Legion . . .
- If you know where the best knoephla soup is, and on what days . . .
- If you can make a hot dish out of any 5 ingredients you have in the cupboard . . .

- If you know not to eat what was cooked in a crockpot at a wild game feed (or at least have a couple Pabsts first) . . .

- If you can't start a conversation without mentioning the weather . . .

Local partisans claim that Doc's Café, Enderlin, serves the best knoephla soup in North Dakota.

- If your answer to "How are you?", "How's the weather?", "How was your crop?", or "How's the ranchin' goin'?" is the same— "Not so bad." . . .

- If your e-mail address is uffda . . .

- If your name is Marlys . . .

- If you routinely end sentences with prepositions, i.e., "Do you want to come with?" . . .

- If the second question after "Where are you from?" is always "Do you know —?" . . .

- If you don't believe you sound like the actors in the movie *Fargo* . . .

- If your nightly TV news includes a weather report from Jay in Glen Ullin . . .

- If you call the Capitol and the Governor answers . . .

- If you use the map's population stats as a restaurant guide . . .

- If you travel over 100 miles to a singles dance . . .

- If you consider somebody stuck up if they don't wave when meeting on the highway . . .
- If your parents knew about your shenanigans before you even reached home . . .
- If you think Jamestown is a big city . . .
- If in winter, you leave your car running in the parking lot while you shop for groceries (or, leave your keys in case anyone needs to borrow it) . . .
- If you can't go for a walk, because people keep stopping to offer you a ride . . .
- If you need your street address and you have to look it up in the phone book . . .
- If you figure, why should you tip the waitress, because she's your cousin . . .
- If attending the funeral of someone in the community is not optional . . .
- If you forget to lock the front door of your home when you leave on a vacation and return six weeks later to find everything in your home undisturbed and just as you left it . . .

Then you must be from North Dakota.

Index

The Pathmaker Series

This work, *Dakota Circle*, is Vol. 1 of the Pathmaker Series issued by the Institute for Regional Studies, North Dakota State University. The Pathmaker Series is a collection of new reflective or creative works that address the question of identity on the Great Plains of North America–who we are in this region, as people and as peoples. The quest for identity in this vast land is a great literary tradition. Wallace Stegner wrote in *Wolf Willow*, "I may not know who I am, but I know where I am from." The Pathmaker Series, then, takes its name from Stegner's essay on "The Making of Paths," in which he dwells upon "the paths that our daily living wore in the prairie." The aim of the series is to follow the paths and help us think about who we are who made them.